THE
MONEY
EDIT

I dedicate this book to my daughters Ire and Teni,
and all my nieces and nephews.
Never give up on your dreams
because great things take time. x

THE MONEY EDIT

*Your no blame, no shame guide
to taking control of your money*

MAKALA GREEN

First published in Great Britain in 2022 by Yellow Kite
An Imprint of Hodder & Stoughton
An Hachette UK company

1

A CIP catalogue record for this title is available from the British Library

Trade Paperback ISBN 978 1 529 39591 4
eBook ISBN 978 1 529 39592 1
Audiobook 978 1 529 39593 8

Typeset in Celeste by Palimpsest Book Production Ltd, Falkirk, Stirlingshire

Printed and bound in Great Britain by Clays Ltd, Elcograf S.p.A.

Hodder & Stoughton policy is to use papers that are natural, renewable and recyclable products and made from wood grown in sustainable forests. The logging and manufacturing processes are expected to conform to the environmental regulations of the country of origin.

Yellow Kite
Hodder & Stoughton Ltd
Carmelite House
50 Victoria Embankment
London EC4Y 0DZ

www.yellowkitebooks.co.uk

CONTENTS

THE FINAL DESTINATION: **YOUR FINANCIAL CHECKLISTS**

PREFACE

Who is this book for?

For many people, one of the greatest fears is financial insecurity.

The Money Edit is for people wanting to overcome financial fear, take control of their money and lead the way to financial freedom. More than ever, people are seeking financial literacy and sometimes, all that is missing are tools, tips and strategies to overcome hurdles and improve overall balance and security. It can often seem insurmountable due to the complexities of financial jargon, along with misconceptions and a plain lack of confidence. Through this book I want to show that with the right mindset and armed with financial knowledge, financial fears can be set aside. *The Money Edit* is for everyone, wherever you are on your financial journey. It will help set you in the right direction with simple route guides. So whether you're just getting started, having a baby, going through a divorce, or retiring, *The Money Edit* will assist you in building a more fulfilling financial future.

The Money Edit is for you if you are:
- Looking for effective ways to manage your money
- Looking to buy your first home
- Starting a family
- Getting started with budgeting
- Aiming to save more money
- Tackling financial debt
- Going through a financial change
- Aiming to build multiple income streams
- Looking to build a money mindset
- Preparing for retirement
- Working towards achieving financial freedom
- Trying to get on track with your finances

Why I wrote it!

I believe it's a serious failing that money management, saving, investing, financial planning or even how to buy a property isn't taught in schools. Instead, we all have to learn as we go along, with little direction. With the increase in population, fewer experienced financial advisers and an ever-changing economy, it's no wonder people so easily lose track of their finances and start wandering around the money maze.

I wrote this book to nurture financial confidence, success and freedom because, with the right skills and necessary financial knowledge, it is attainable for everyone. The world would certainly feel a more comfortable place if everyone was in tune with their finances and had improved relationships with money. I aim to do away with the myths that finance is boring and complicated. This book shows that managing money can be fun by offering a fresh way to look at money, providing warnings about financial potholes, and offering redirection should anyone take a wrong turn and get off track. Managing money can be overwhelming when you don't have the know-how.

The Money Edit contains all the tips, tools, knowledge and strategies you need to grow confidence and take control.

What this book expects to accomplish

No-jargon, straightforward, effective guidance, along with basic principles, can take the fear out of finance, change money attitudes and be the foundation of the road to financial freedom.

The book explores a diverse range of financial subject matters. I believe all the information to be accurate, but the book does not and is not intended to provide individualised or tailored advice. It does mean, though, that should you seek personal input from a financial adviser, you will know exactly what you're asking for and be able to easily recognise the difference between the good, the bad and the absolutely inadvisable.

How to use it

As with any journey, it starts with planning how to get there, which routes and roads to take. If you have a clear picture of what the destination looks like, it's easier to know where you are heading, if you're going in the right direction and, most importantly, when you have arrived. As life coach Anthony Robbins says, 'The way we represent things in our minds determines how we feel about life.' Money is no exception, and the financial journey we face is not much different. The first step is to start and then navigate through to the end. Each chapter takes a step-by-step approach to develop the money mindset, improve financial literacy and boost financial confidence. Each chapter ends with a chapter summary to allow you to discover ways to progress financially.

Life can be hectic and unpredictable, and MONEY often takes centre stage. *The Money Edit* provides a no blame or shame insight to help you work on areas that need improvement as well as sharpen money skills you have already mastered. It will also prove a useful resource to refer back to at any point on your financial journey. The approach is simple, informative and practical and is based on the issues and experiences of my many clients over the years. I have covered all the financial choices you may encounter on the journey, the decisions you need to make, and the signs and signals to keep you on the straight and narrow.

PART 1 will encourage you to be comfortable and open with money to help overcome any financial fears and manage your money with confidence. It focuses on understanding the money mindset and other factors that can affect our money decisions, such as emotions.

PART 2 provides insightful information on tracking income and expenses like a pro to create room for saving – something we struggle with as a nation. It delves into various routes to achieve passive income. It will help you start the journey of building a dream future, covering saving, buying property and being aware of borrowing so you can spot the good, the bad and the ugly that can often throw many off course.

PART 3 talks about changing circumstances, because every journey is bound to have a hitch or two. It identifies scenarios such as marriage, moving home or having a baby and solutions to ride the bumps and still achieve financial success, regardless of what life has thrown at us.

PART 4 navigates through the ins and outs of retirement planning. It delves into all the stages you need to consider, from planning your dream retirement and looking at alternative retirement routes, to the know-how of retiring securely – so you can enjoy every minute.

FINALLY, at the end of the book you will find useful resources to help arrive at your dream destination in style, including a comprehensive financial checklist and other financial planning tools to help you pinpoint your progress, explore how far you have travelled on your financial journey, and drive forward in areas you need to tackle further.

ABOUT ME

Where do I begin? There is so much to tell . . .

My journey with money began when I was around five and loved nothing more than counting the hundreds of pennies my dad would save for me. That Tesco bag, heavy with coins, was so exciting; I found it fascinating that the clinking contents of that carrier could be counted into neatly stacked piles and exchanged for pounds – with so much more spending potential. Opening my first bank account at seven was momentous, and I was green with envy that the lucky ladies behind the bank's glass screens were able to count coins all day (little did I know that would become my pet hate in years to come).

I grew up on an East London council estate with my mother and siblings, a world away, I'm well aware, from the wealthy clients I advise today. Despite this, my parents worked extremely hard to give me everything and taught me to appreciate all things – especially money, which my parents instilled in me wasn't just for spending; more importantly, it was for saving. That really stuck with me, although it wasn't until my early teens that I appreciated what they meant, in particular, 'If you want financial freedom you have to earn it!' Luckily that was exactly what I was prepared to do.

I got my first Saturday job at 14, working 8am to 6pm in a hairdresser (that probably wouldn't be allowed today!), for which I was paid £20 for the day. It didn't take me long to realise it wasn't just about the money but also about time and value. I figured I could earn the same (or more) in fewer hours, so at 15 I decided to go out on my own. My dad was still giving me pocket money; little did he know I wasn't spending any of it. I was making hundreds of pounds doing hair during lunch breaks and on weekends. At the time, I didn't look at it as a business – it was fun, I was in demand because I had the skills, and because I was earning an income through my own hard work, I was quite happy to spend some of it, especially as I knew that in the meantime the pocket money was mounting up nicely. Going weekly to the bank to deposit my money brought me as much satisfaction as that Tesco bag of coins, and it wasn't that long before I'd saved my first £1,000.

I left school at 16 with high hopes of becoming a doctor, and after leaving school with 9 GCSEs, I had my pick of sixth-form colleges. I decided to study psychology and sociology at A Level, but my time at college was short-lived. A friend of mine, Chloe, told me that at my age I could get a job in a bank, which I never quite believed. Nevertheless, I typed up my CV, sent it out to several high-street banks and endlessly practised interview skills with my sister. To my astonishment, I found they all got back to me; I was spoiled for choice. I started work as a cashier and, even on my first day, was exposed to so much money and responsibility that childhood memories came flooding back, along with the importance of appreciation. I worked hard, never guessing that in time I would be able to change the way people thought and felt about money and offer advice that could change lives. Now I was the person behind the glass screen, and I loved it. The role of a cashier taught me a lot, and it also introduced me to the world of debt and other issues. I'd always assumed money made everyone as happy as it did me; I grew to understand that was only the case when money was managed well. I soon discovered the impact on every aspect of life and relationships when it wasn't.

After two years of cashiering, I felt it was time to come out from behind the screen; I wanted to help with money problems. I became a personal banker, a qualified mortgage adviser, and hit my dream role as a qualified financial adviser by the age of 21. I was able to bring all I'd learned from previous roles and use that experience and leverage to change lives for the better, from day-to-day problems to helping individuals, couples and families buy their first home. I had a practical understanding of client needs, which helped me stand out from other financial advisers. Added to that was the fact I was young, female and Black – all three of which were unheard of in the world of finance.

By the time I was 19, I'd saved enough to buy my first property, testimony to the benefits of hard work and savings. By my mid-twenties, I was married with two daughters and was determined, despite the challenges, to balance family life with my passion for making a financial difference.

I set up my own successful financial practice at the age of 28 and was the first black female associate partner in the billion-pound FTSE 100 wealth management company. It was then that I discovered the real challenges that many people face when it comes to money, and how guilt, shame and lack of financial knowledge can so easily swallow your financial goals and dreams if you are not careful.

I have had the pleasure of working with individuals, business owners and corporate companies to bring them the success and security they enjoy today. I have also enjoyed presenting at over a hundred events to share my financial knowledge.

In 2019 came one of the proudest moments of my life when I was recognised as the first Black female chartered financial planner in the UK, one of the highest qualifications achievable in the industry. For me, it was a joy just to finally graduate, something I had always wanted to do. The added bonus is that I now use this badge of honour to encourage more young women into the world of finance – because it's not as scary as it seems!

I later used this platform to set up The Wealth Check, a coaching company that helps individuals and business owners – wherever they are in their journey – to overcome pre-held views and get on financial track. I have opened the world of finance up to a much younger audience, making financial planning accessible, fun and jargon free.

In 2021 I was awarded Financial Adviser of the Year for South East England by the prestigious *Professional Adviser*. It felt surreal, although heart-warming to know that my efforts, hard work and perseverance over the last 17 years has not been in vain. I dedicated the award to all young women who aspire to be leaders in their fields and to make a difference in the world. In the same year I was selected as one of the 67 women to feature in *The Female Lead Volume II: We Rise By Lifting Others* (The Female Lead are a charity who inspire better change for millions of girls and women). I was noted as one of the most admirable and inspirational woman across the world of finance.

It's been a rewarding journey, and I have loved every minute of it. But I am ready to take it to another level and to help the nation discover new ways of looking at money with the financial confidence they need to achieve their highest aspirations.

PART 1

MONEY TRACKING

It's the most basic, fundamental part of our everyday lives and impacts even the most mundane decisions. It underpins our financial goals and has the power to affect the way we think and feel. And yet it remains the oldest taboo and makes us cringe every time we say the word 'money'.

CHAPTER 1

NO BLAME NO SHAME

*Let's talk about it, get comfortable with it,
remove the shame around it, and make money
a positive part of our everyday lives.*

If I ask you how you feel about MONEY, what is the first thing you think of?

It may take a while to answer, and that's okay. The truth is there is no one answer to this question as we all have different views, experiences and money values. For some, money can be a dirty word, and they can't bear to say it aloud. In contrast, others may relish just the thought of money and can't stop talking about it.

We can agree that money affects us all, and our mentality towards money shapes the world we live in. So, it's fair to say money has huge importance in our everyday lives. So why do we lack confidence when dealing with money and feel uncomfortable talking about it? According to the Money and Pensions Service (MaPS), 39% of adults (20.3 million) don't feel confident managing their money, and 63% feel they can't determine what happens in their lives when it comes to money and have little sense of control over it. This is the pinnacle of why I'm so passionate about helping you make money work for you.

We all know how meaningful it is to talk about money, but why do we give ourselves such a hard time? One of the reasons is that we are taught to believe that money is maths, and so if you're not good at maths, you can't be good with money. This is not true. The way we manage our money has more to do with psychology – the way we think and feel rather than how we deal with calculations and spreadsheets. It has been said that the way we treat money is influenced less by logic and more by embedded beliefs that we are unaware exist.

The majority of us are happy to discuss fashion, love, politics or religion, but we shy away from money. For most, just the thought of discussing their bank statement or savings (or lack of) fuels shame, embarrassment and vulnerability. It's almost as if discussing our financial affairs is illegitimate, preventing us from sharing how we truly feel due to fear of judgement. You are not alone. I'm here to tell you that this is normal, but I do want to break the chain of those money myths and misconceptions. Money doesn't have to be the topic of every discussion, but you should realise it's okay to be open and discuss it when you need to, and not hide away from it.

Life can throw all sorts of things our way, and society puts a lot of pressure on our financial standing. For example, take the conventional timeline: we are expected to graduate from university, find a good job, buy a home, get married, start a family, and retire in a methodical timescale and order. Too often, these timelines completely contradict the normal narrative known as *real life*; you may get married, then buy a home or start a family and then graduate – and that's okay. The feeling of failing to live up to society's financial standards can cause psychological discomfort, disappointment and despair. The obstacles that prevent us from having more money are implanted in the emotional, psychological and spiritual circumstances that frame how we think. So, it's time to create your own standards and develop a new way of thinking so you can create a more fulfilling future with financial freedom and balance.

Focus on your money feelings

Money is intertwined with almost every goal in life; therefore, it seems natural to blame money when things don't go to plan. In fact, it's much deeper than money; it's your mindset that defines your decisions with money. If you want to improve your financial wellbeing, you need to get up close and personal with your feelings. If you really want something, the likelihood is that you will do everything to get it, regardless of whether you have the money.

Have you ever experienced genuinely wanting something, whether a handbag, an outfit or a holiday, and your mind is telling you, *yes*, but your money is telling you *no* (you don't have enough!). The mind is so powerful it can convince you that your wants are needs, and even if the credit card foots the bill, you've got to have it. So it's not money that gets us into problems but our mindsets and how we think.

However intensely painful or pleasant your experience with money has been, the good news is that you can change your relationship at any time. The next chapter explores changing the way we think and feel about money. That might mean letting go of those societal standards and living a life that's right for you, so you don't feel unnecessary financial pressures. (See Chapter 2: Mind Over Money.)

What's money got to do with it?

What do stress, worry and anxiety have in common? You guessed it: money, whether it's anxiety about paying bills, the guilt of overspending or feelings of disappointment over your income. Whether you have a lot of money or a little, you are still likely to worry about it or suffer from money shame and guilt. An online survey by YouGov found that 25% of UK adults said they felt guilty about their money problems, 41% felt embarrassed, and 28% didn't talk about these problems with anyone.

Many people suffer from financial worry in silence, burying their heads in the sand and hoping their problems will wash away. I totally understand your frustrations; the society we live in does not provide any rule books when it comes to money, and therefore it's difficult to know when you are heading in the right direction and when you are going off course.

If you want to move forward in your financial journey, I will need your input to make this work. You need to get comfortable with money and be open to talking about it, even if that's just with yourself. According to MaPS, for 59% of life events working-age adults face they did not seek financial help. Imagine if we ignored our health the way we do with our money? We have all had moments where we felt embarrassed about our health or wellbeing, but on the whole, we all understand the importance of seeking medical advice if we are sick. Although you may not see the physical deterioration with money, it's no different, and the effects are just as damaging.

So, let's talk about it, get comfortable with it, remove the shame around it, and make money a positive part of our everyday lives.

> *Money can't solve your problems*
> *if your head is not in the right place.*

The past is the past, but the present is powerful

I've said this before, and I'll say it again: you have to learn to forgive yourself for your past financial mistakes; you can't change them. It's normal to be frustrated, but it's time to use that frustration to spark your financial future, goals and dreams. For example, if you have debt, a natural reaction is to worry about how quickly you can pay it off, which can cause anxiety that may contradict your goal. Instead, you can focus on training the mind not to take on any more debt, a much more powerful method that will leave you feeling more focused and in control. I know this is easier said than done; that's why I aim to support you through overcoming your frustrations throughout this book. You will find the Financial Affirmations section in the next chapter (see page 37) useful to help you recognise you are not defined by your past, and you can improve your financial future right now.

> *The past is your lesson,*
> *The present is your gift,*
> *The future is your motivation.*

Financial fortunes over flaws

It's easy to get bogged down with your flaws and forget about everything you have accomplished. When was the last time you told yourself, 'I'm proud of myself', regardless of what you achieved, whether it was buying your first home, saving an emergency fund or sticking to your budget at the supermarket? You have to give yourself credit; it's likely that no one else will, not because you're undeserving of praise but because few people have substantial knowledge of your financial affairs. Use the Money Mindfulness section in the next chapter (see page 23) to list the financial successes or fortunes that you have achieved, or are planning to achieve.

Money mistakes can lead to better money management

If we never make mistakes, we don't learn. We learn from our experiences, whether good or bad. I understand that we never want to have bad lessons with money, but it can be useful to use your money mishaps to improve the way you manage your finances. Money issues are widespread, with nearly 27% of people in the UK struggling to pay bills or rent.

Look back to the last time you made a poor decision or had a bad experience with money (if any). Think about what your behaviour was like and why you made the choices you did, and how you can now change those behaviours and your thinking to improve your financial choices and outcomes. People who continually get in debt don't have 'issues' with money; they just continue to repeat the same mistakes without questioning, challenging or changing their behaviours or money mindset.

So, how can you avoid those mistakes from happening again?

Think of some of the mishaps that hurt or affected you most. What would you do differently now that would forge a more positive outcome? It might not happen overnight, but if you get used to analysing your behaviours and money mindset, rather than just focusing on money, you will gradually improve your relationship with money.

> *Money + Mistakes = Human*

Relationship is key
Think about a relationship – what does it require to work? Although not everyone will have the same ideas and views, there are some unquestionable ingredients that bind a relationship together, such as investing time, love, dedication and commitment. Most would agree that making sacrifices is key; you may not agree or like everything within the relationship, but you compromise because your desire for the relationship outweighs the flaws. Your relationship with money is no different; it requires you to invest time, love and dedication and make sacrifices to maintain financial stability – the secret recipe to riches.

I understand it may not always be plain sailing, but the right money mindset can provide the balance your boat needs to sail your way to financial freedom. Instead of allowing money to take control of your life, which is not healthy in any relationship, take charge. You don't have to be at war with money; it's time to make peace with your bank statements, savings and debts. Just remember, the harder the battle, the sweeter the victory.

Small money is still money
Financial progress doesn't always have to be immense or Instagrammable. Making progress with money and your goals often means taking small steps consistently; in fact, consistency is one

of the most important factors. Many of us give up or fail to start on our dreams because we feel they are too small and not worthy. Be patient, and don't be afraid to take small steps or pocket your pennies, because it will transform into sizeable success. What actions can you start taking right now to help you advance in achieving your future financial goals?

Put aside perfection

The goal isn't perfection; it's progress. Celebrate the little wins as well as the big wins – even celebrate your failures and losses because that's how you learn. When it comes to managing your money, don't make perfection the enemy of progress. There are many opinions out there, such as 'buying a home is better than renting', 'you have to be rich to invest' or 'you have to earn well before you can save'. These are all myths and can prevent you from achieving your personal financial goals. Instead, you should celebrate each accomplishment, no matter how big or small. You can use a goals priority list (see page 282), which will be incredibly valuable in meeting your money goals; it might be that you finally took out that life insurance policy you've been putting off, set up a savings account to build a property deposit, or created a will. It is still an achievement, and the sense of progression will motivate you to keep up the momentum and do more.

Therapy is money medicine

Speaking with a therapist, financial expert, family member or friend can help iron out some of your money worries and remove some of the stigmas of shame that sadly surrounds money. According to a survey conducted by Perks in 2019, money is the biggest cause of stress among employed adults: 56% worried about not having enough emergency funds to cover unexpected costs, 41% felt they were financially behind compared to their peers, and 39% felt unable to reach their future financial goals, such as buying a home.

Suppose you have made numerous attempts to improve your

finances, and you still can't make head or tail of them. In that case, it might be worth speaking with a professional, such as a therapist, money coach or financial adviser, to help eliminate some of the financial burdens, whether it's controlling your spending habits, dealing with unhealthy attitudes towards money or unpicking problematic childhood experiences.

The main thing is that you feel in control of your money, and that you have the confidence to make the right choices to lead you to your financial destiny. It is important that you understand there is no perfect way to your journey with money, but it should be unique to you and free of guilt, shame and judgement. Get familiar with monitoring your money habits, questioning yourself before making unusual purchases or rectifying sudden changes in money patterns. You will be amazed at what a difference you can make in your financial journey by being open and embracing more financial positivity, preparation and planning.

Now that we have got that off our chest, let the financial transformation begin!

> *You are the change your money craves;*
> *I know it, and, in your heart, you know it too!*

CHAPTER 2

MIND OVER MONEY

> 'Money is only a tool. It will take you
> wherever you wish, but it will not
> replace you as the driver.'
> —Ayn Rand

Want to know the difference between a successful person and one that struggles financially? Simply, it is their money mindset. Your money mindset constitutes the feelings and thoughts you subconsciously develop towards money from your life experiences or childhood memories. These thoughts control your actions and financial decisions. A negative money mindset can create barriers in your financial journey. However, with simple regular practices, you can easily develop a positive money mindset that will help shape your road to financial freedom.

Money, money, money

There is no escaping money: we all use it; spend it, earn it and hopefully save it! And no matter how much we have, we naturally want more! We all have different perceptions of money, but the bottom line is money is simply a legal tender or a promise to pay to buy goods and services. Yet it means so much more in our daily lives; in fact, money can be so powerful it can influence our behaviours, mindset, social interactions and society as a whole. So, you can see why it is important to understand what money means to you so you can take the lead and manage it. Money can allow you to live the life of your dreams. Likewise, if you're not careful, money can be a living nightmare; it can ruin friendships and relationships and cause depression.

There's an intertwined relationship between our money and our environment, which affects both our physical and mental state. Money plays a vital role in our everyday lives, whether it's love, health, career or business. It can create an emotional imbalance if not effectively managed, which can lead you to feel guilt or shame and prevent you from expressing how you really feel. The truth is there are no rights, or wrongs when it comes to money, but taking responsibility for your actions and making time to manage your money well will certainly set you on the right path to financial security, wellness and freedom.

What does money mean to me?

Money is not simply money. If it were, our 'money problems' would be easily solved. We could just stop spending more, and everything would be okay!

To understand the problems we experience with money in adulthood, we must go back to our early years and explore the meaning of money in our own lives and the lives of our parents. The attitudes our parents had about money more than likely shaped the attitudes we hold today. Take these sayings for example: 'Money is the root of all evil', 'The rich get richer, and the poor get poorer' or 'Money doesn't grow on trees'. Do they ring any bells?

We all have a relationship with money, whether we like it or not. So why not learn how to understand your money beliefs and values to help you make better, informed choices. If you are in a relationship, you also need to come to terms with your partner's attitudes – not to mention those of their parents (see Chapter 7: Money and Marriage).

What did money represent in your family when you were growing up, and what were you taught about its uses?

- Do thoughts of money bring up feelings of worry, guilt, anger, sadness, power, love or joy?

- Did your parents fight about money? Did they use money to control you or one another? Or use money to show love?
- Do you feel grateful for the money you have earned or acquired?
- How do you decide how or when to spend it?
- Do you give a portion of your earnings back to charity or your community?

The answers to these questions can set you on the path to understanding how your emotions influence your spending patterns. Now think about and write down what money means to you:

1. Money is _____
2. Money is _____
3. Money is _____

> *It isn't the money that matters,*
> *it's how you use it that determines*
> *its true value.*

Mindset over money

Many people believe that if they were rich, life would be uncomplicated, but this is not true. A rich person with a poor mindset can easily waste their riches without understanding quite how the money departed so drastically. While you may wonder how a person from humble beginnings can rise to success overnight, well, they likely possessed a rich mindset! If you tell yourself, 'I'll never pay off my debts' or 'What's the point in saving, I'll never be rich', then you are setting yourself up to fail. Turn any pessimistic thoughts into positive ones and see the difference in your behaviour towards money. Building a rich mindset will cost you nothing, and so it's a good way to start your financial journey or reconnect to it. If you take the time to get your money mindset right first, the rest will naturally follow.

Money + Time = Value

For me, it all started with counting those pennies. Subconsciously, this was where my journey started in valuing money. I quickly learned that pennies became pounds and pounds became hundreds and realised all money had value, even a penny.

It's never about how much money you have or earn, but how you value it. If money has little or no value to you, the amount you earn is immaterial. You won't see the worth, and therefore it will quickly go to waste – one of the main reasons rich people go broke or become unhappy. Ever heard of the term 'more money, more problems'? This is prevalent when there is no value for money.

The concept of money + time = value suggests the disparity between people who want money now and don't consider the future, and those who believe in compounding to achieve a greater value in the future. What you do with your money over time will determine its true value. If you consistently spend, your future value will likely be less than what you started with. Alternatively, if you save and invest over time, your value is likely to be more than the original sum. We all have different perceptions of money, but the bottom line is the more you value money, the higher your chances of increasing financial success.

'Time will take your money,
but money won't buy time.'
—JAMES TAYLOR

Money mindfulness

Sometimes we feel worried, nervous, or financially overwhelmed. When this happens, I like to sit down and do this little exercise. It's one of the easiest ways to remind myself how blessed and fortunate I am. It was my mum that taught me to count my blessings, no matter how small. I truly believe that we are happiest when we learn to appreciate the simple things, and so doing this little daily task will help you achieve the money mindfulness you need and help you be grateful for things you have. Write down five things that you are grateful for: they can be things you're happy about in your life, the amazing day you've had, the people you love, or who make you laugh, or who make you feel safe. They can be really big things like your home or really small things like catching up with friends or your mum's tasty Sunday dinner.

THINGS I AM GRATEFUL FOR RIGHT NOW:

1. God: I am thankful for many blessings, and I know that without him, nothing is possible.
2. My family: My two beautiful girls, my handsome hubby and my larger family, especially my mum and dad, sisters, brothers, nieces and nephews who all mean the world to me!
3. My cheerleaders: Those who have supported my journey – you know who you are!
4. My health: Health is wealth!
5. My house: I have worked to make a home that is my safe place, my recharge hub and a place of good food and laughter.

NOW LIST SOME OF YOURS:

1. _____

2. _____

3. --

4. --

5. --

FINANCIAL GOAL SETTING

We all like to be challenged in life, and we do this by setting ourselves goals and targets. The first step to setting a goal is figuring out what matters to you and discovering your interests and skills. You may have always dreamed of becoming a doctor, travelling the world or owning your very own mansion. Whatever it may be, it's likely to have a price tag attached. Therefore, you must put a good plan in place and be prepared to make some sacrifices to make it happen. A plan will provide a route to your end destination and give you structure and discipline to shape your life. If you go about life without a plan, it's very easy to find yourself lost mentally, financially and physically. Setting goals is a must-do, regardless of your age, status or background. By remaining dedicated, you can almost guarantee your goals will become a reality in future.

Give your goal some legs

Too often, it's not money that holds us back from attaining our goals but our inner thoughts and limitations. Changing my attitude towards money and supporting my goals definitely helped me transform financially, and I know it can for you too. Goals with successful outcomes require support, whether from you, a friend or family. For example, if you want to retire at fifty you'll need to support this goal by contributing enough to a pension or some asset to provide an income in the future. Try noting one thing you can do every day that will lead you towards your goals.

It's a goal!

Part of success is understanding when you have achieved and accomplished great things. If you are that person who is really hard on yourself when you fail, then you need to make an exceptional effort to praise yourself when you do well. It will leave you with a taster of success and will have you wanting more. So don't be cautious in your celebrations when they are due or wait for a sizeable success before you pat yourself on the back. Success has no measure; it can be small or great. Try to get into the habit of congratulating yourself on goals achieved daily. It may be as simple as walking to work instead of driving the car and saving some fuel money. You may be surprised by how many successes you achieve regularly.

Let's goal get it!

Besides giving you financial confidence, motivation and empowerment, I want this book to inspire you to dream. Do you have a vision for the lifestyle you want to live but no idea how to get there? Or perhaps you have a plan, but after years of hard work, you don't have much to show for it. Either can be frustrating and demoralising, but tomorrow is a new day, and I'm here to show you how to reach your financial goals. So please go ahead and list your goals below. Remember to aim high, dream big, and be financially fearless. I honestly believe you can achieve anything you put your mind to. Don't feel overwhelmed if it seems a bit much to start with; you can revisit these goal-setting pages whenever you feel ready. Here are some examples you may want to consider:

- Get out of debt – completely!
- Build an emergency fund
- Plan for early retirement
- Save a deposit for a property
- Buy your first home
- Go on a Caribbean cruise

- Take the family on holiday
- Create multiple incomes
- Pay for children's education
- Renovate your home
- Buy a mansion
- Live on less than you earn
- Reduce or eliminate poor financial habits
- End a costly addiction
- Live abroad
- Buy a sports car

You may also want to think of your goals in terms of those you *need* to achieve and those you *dream* of achieving.

MY NEED GOALS	MY DREAM GOALS
•	•
•	•
•	•
•	•
•	•

A goal is a dream with a deadline!

Create a timeline for your goals

They say a goal is a dream with a deadline, but timescales must be realistic. Allocate a timescale that works for you to each goal you have set. Some will naturally be longer than others. Goals can range from daily goals to weekly, monthly, quarterly, half-yearly or yearly ones. For example, micro-goals may fall into the daily or weekly category, whereas buying a car may fall into a half-yearly goal and buying a house will more than likely fall into a yearly goal as it may take several years to save up for a deposit on a house. Your timeline will give you the confidence you need to work toward your financial goals at a steady pace.

How to achieve your financial goals

Setting goals is just the start of a great financial plan, but action, perseverance and discipline are at the heart of achieving them. Look at the goals that you have set on your list above. Do they scare you a little, excite you a lot or maybe a bit of both? I've found that you can make your invisible dreams come to life by setting visible goals and giving yourself a deadline. Take it step by step in approaching your goals and break them down into more manageable chunks. Goals need to be measurable because this allows you to track your progress at any given time. It also provides you with a clear idea as to whether your strategy is working or not. The easiest way to do this is to assign a monetary figure and timescale to your goal. For example:

- **Immeasurable goal:** to save up for a mortgage deposit one day.
- **Measurable goal:** to save up to £15,340 for a mortgage deposit in five years.

OK, so now you've established your goal, you've made it specific, and you've made it measurable. Now you need to break it into smaller parts. Doing so will make your journey a lot easier because you'll know precisely what actionable steps you need to take to get there. And on top of that, your goal is far less likely to be daunting.

GENERATE BITE-SIZED GOALS

Studies have proven that the further away your set goal is, the less likely you will achieve it. You may lose focus, lose enthusiasm or believe it's less likely to happen. In addition, your circumstances may change, which may mean you have to change the original goal. So, while big goals are still beneficial, you can reap the rewards much quicker with smaller goals. You may have a goal to save £5,000 to clear some debts. You may find it easier to put away £13.70 a day (for one year), than find £5,000 as one lump sum. Likewise, if you run your own business, instead of waiting for the taxman to drop the bombshell of what you owe, there's probably less heartache in putting aside about 20% of your earnings each month.

Linking back to the mortgage goal, let's say your goal is to save up to £15,340 for a mortgage in five years. Your first step would be to calculate how much you need to save per year and then per month (see below). It will help you control your spending habits and budget appropriately.

- £15,340 ÷ 5 (years) = £3,068 per year
- £3,068 ÷ 12 (months) = £256 per month

Now suddenly, saving up for £15,340 seems a lot less challenging!

Here are some examples of other bite-sized goals you may consider:

- Pay off one credit card (see credit card section for further details)
- Open an emergency fund savings account
- Set up a pension/contribute a bit more than last year
- Open a Lifetime ISA and contribute to it (see Chapter 4: The Savings Journey)
- Decorate a room in your house
- Cut back on one takeaway per week

- Reduce the amount spent on cigarettes/alcohol
- Save £100 per month for your child's education (after 18 years that would equate to £21,600 excluding interest)
- Plan a staycation
- Buy a share of a house (see Chapter 6: Property)
- Spend less than you earn
- Avoid going overdrawn
- Make money from items no longer needed
- Travel abroad
- Buy an economical car instead of a fancy sports car

KEEP AN EYE ON YOUR GOALS

Over time, things will change in different aspects of your life, and therefore your goals may change as a result. Regularly review your goal plans to make sure they coincide with your future requirements. Whatever the goal is, make sure it is achievable and be fair to yourself with what you can realistically achieve. Remain focused, enthusiastic and consistent with your goals; the more goals you accomplish, the more confident you will become in being financially astute.

Having a goal plan is your safety net to effective financial planning. Remember, once you have achieved a set goal, get back to the drawing board and plan again. Never stop planning! Any time you go through a change or set a new goal, be sure to raise your standards. Without limiting your beliefs, allow yourself to dream bigger than you ever have before.

NEEDS VS WANTS

It's easy to be influenced by what others think and to strive for gratification from them. But it's important that your goals are your own and nobody else's. Being driven will help keep you focused and on track, so it's important to be honest with yourself and write down what would truly be beneficial to you by establishing your needs vs wants. Jot down as many needs and wants as you can think of for the next five years.

Prioritise your financial goals
PRIORITIES KILL PROBLEMS

- What's important to you right now?
- What will be necessary for you in future?
- Do you live for the here and now and struggle to see beyond?

If only we could wave a magic wand to solve all our money problems, we'd all be free from financial worry and stress. Well, prioritising is the magic wand when it comes to financial planning. Identifying your priorities is critical, whether it's clearing debts, buying your first house, travelling or buying a car. Understanding your needs will help you make the necessary changes to handle your money correctly. Prioritising means putting yourself and your goals first. It may mean sacrificing some things you enjoy, such as regular nights out with friends, buying designer clothes or going on luxury vacations. All of those are well and good if you have enough money to fund this lifestyle, but if not, you could be putting your future finances at risk. It is funny how something can mean so much now but have little to no relevance in the future. So be wise with what you spend your money on and aim to make room for your future goals. Take a moment to think about what you would like to achieve over the next five years and list them in order of priority. Alongside your personal goals you may want to factor in your family, career and business goals.

Don't be overwhelmed by the mountain you have to climb, instead just focus on the small, actionable steps you can take every day. You *can* do it, but it starts from prioritising your goals . . . so go get 'em! It's time to put your financial goals in order (use the goal priorities list on page 282 to help you).

Try answering the following questions:

What would it mean to you to achieve your goals?

How would you feel once you have achieved your goals?

Once you have listed your short- and long-term goals, consider how they will impact your future income and expenditure. Are you expecting a promotion, do you plan on going part-time, moving abroad or giving up smoking or alcohol? Listing how your goals will affect your budgeting will give you the financial advantage you need to take your finances to the next level.

 FOR A PERSONAL VIEW: Complete the goal priorities list (see page 282)

> *'Needs are imposed by nature,*
> *wants are sold by society.'*
> —MOKOKOMA MOKHONOANA

FINANCIAL VISIONING

Since as early as childhood, I have been fascinated with cutting things out and sticking them together. My mother was a tailor, so I grew up surrounded by pictures of fashion magazines, dress patterns and sewing machines. Fast-forward a few years, and my creative daydreams have become one of the most financially transforming practices: vision boarding. This successful method will bring your dreams to life and help you achieve your most desired goals.

Do you want to:

1. Live a life that represents you?
2. Live a life that releases your full potential?
3. Create a life that will outlive you?

'Yes!', I hear you screaming. You are not alone. Popular celebrities and influential people swear by the vision board method and its power of manifestation. There's just something about putting your goals and visions on paper that connects with the law of attraction and helps bring them to life. Psychologists have proven that vision boards help increase motivation, confidence and even performance. The most exciting part is visualising those goals – imagining your wildest dreams can be lots of fun!

Vision boards can be based on a singular idea, multiple ideas, or a theme. Overall, they look at the bigger picture of what you might want the future to look like. They can include a new dream home, holiday, kicking a bad habit or becoming a money magnet; there really are no limits. Brian Tracy, a world-renowned motivational speaker, states, 'A clear vision backed by definite plans gives a tremendous feeling of confidence and personal power.'

Three steps to designing the life of your dreams

This simple, effective three-step process to creating a vision board will help you bring your visions to life and create a structure you can monitor every step of the way.

- **Use the Power of Choice** Have you ever made a poor decision, whether to do with money, a relationship, or a pair of expensive shoes? We've all been there. But with every decision you make, there is a choice, and you are in charge of the choices that will lead to your destiny, dreams and goals. So take charge of your plans. Say, for instance, you want to earn £100,000, but you are currently earning £30,000. Ask yourself what it will take to get there. It may take some reprogramming of the mind, realigning your plans, mingling in the right circles and being committed and focused. Your thinking becomes you; every decision you make in life affects your future. So go ahead and reinvent yourself – *you don't get in life what you want. You get in life what you are and the changes you are willing to make.*

- **Use the Power of Visualisation** Have you ever set out to do something and then told yourself you couldn't? You must believe you can make it happen! What gets you out of bed every morning? You may have a goal in mind but try describing exactly what it looks like. For example, if it's a home, picture the walls, the flooring, the decor, the furnishings and how you feel in the house. Define how you want to feel about your finances in five years and what attitudes you will change and develop to get there. You need to expand yourself and let go of any limiting beliefs, including toxic people or things that you have allowed to restrict you.

- **Use the Power of Commitment** Have you ever set a goal and given up or thrown the towel in? 'It's too hard', 'I can't do it', 'it's not for me' is what we often tell ourselves. Well, the next time a thought like this tries to enter a room in

your brain, you tell it, 'I can, I will, and I deserve to achieve.'
Just watch how fast that thought will run out.

Once vision goals have been set, you need to stick at them and
see them through to the end. Lists are a great way of remembering
your needs and ensuring you achieve them. Without a list, it's
easy to get lost with all the other temptations around. Just think
about how successful a shopping trip is with a shopping list
compared to without. You easily forget what you set out for and
end up buying everything else but the items you originally went
in the store for. This principle also applies to everyday life. By
setting and listing goals, it helps keep you focused on what you
need to achieve. It also prevents you from losing direction.

Create your financial vision board

Creating a vision board will give you the motivation you need to
adopt better money habits. It will include all the things you want
to achieve in a visual format. It may consist of pictures, magazines,
internet photos or drawings. Your financial vision board will help
remind you to stay on track with your financial goals. It should
change each year or be amended to ensure your incentives remain
fresh and inspiring. However, before you start with your vision
board, it's important to dig a bit deeper to discover your genuine
goals so you can maximise your full potential.

A vision board works best when it is somewhere where you
can see it every day. We are human and we need a constant
reminder to cement things into the brain. It may be your fridge,
wardrobe, or the back of your front door; but the key is visibility.

MONEY MOTTO

To make your vision boards more powerful, you can add money
mottos, sayings and phrases that represent your beliefs around
money. Money mottoes can help improve your money mindset
and transform the way you think and feel about money, and so
you should mentally carry them wherever you go to form a

constant reminder of what is yet to come. Here is a list of some money mottoes to get you started:

- I am financially worthy
- I am wealthy
- Financial freedom is for me

MANY HAVE SIGHT, BUT FEW HAVE VISION

Helen Keller proudly stated: 'The only thing that is worse than being blind is having sight but no vision.' Financial visioning plays a key part in giving you the motivation you need to achieve your financial goals. Once you accomplish them, they will elevate your quality of life. To put it simply, how much happier would you be if you could buy your first home or pay off your mortgage? Or afford to go on exotic holidays every year? Or even just not have to worry about bills every day? Draw or attach the things you want to financially achieve. It doesn't have to be a work of art; it's mainly to help you bring some life to your future achievements. Here is an example of a financial vision board, but you should make yours personal to you.

FINANCIAL VISION BOARD

HAPPINESS
Financial Wellbeing
Start a Family
Buy a house
Set up a business
Buy a dream car
Travel around asia
PROSPERITY
FINACIAL FREEDOM
Exercise regularly
Read more books
DREAM BIG
INSPIRE

Now it's your turn to have a go. Don't panic if you can't think of much to start with. I hope after completing this book, you will have lots to add. Alternatively, feel free to offload all your ideas, dreams and desires no matter how big or small on the table below, and remember that what you dream about now may change as you get older, and that's okay!

MY FINANCIAL VISION BOARD				
	PERSONAL	CAREER/ BUSINESS	FAMILY	DREAM
TWENTIES				
THIRTIES				
FORTIES				
FIFTIES				
SIXTIES				
BEYOND				

FINANCIAL AFFIRMATIONS

It's time to open new doors, build new bridges, remove financial stress and give yourself a new sense of confidence, security and freedom. Just think of where you are *now* and where you could be in five years. Start every month and week with an affirmation to keep you financially elevated. By believing in yourself and realising your self-worth, you will be surprised what you can achieve. Your financial mistakes do not bind you, and a few bad directions do not mean you are financially lost. You are enough, and you have what it takes to eliminate financial fears and achieve financial freedom. Here are some examples:

- My money goals will manifest this year
- I attract wealth and abundance
- I am worthy of financial security
- Debt is a thing of the past
- I am on the road to financial freedom
- My income is increasing daily
- Financial success is mine
- I am a money magnet
- I am wealthy
- I am ready for abundance
- I deserve to be financially free

Try to list five money mantras you can use to be a positive daily reminder:

1. _____

2. _____

3. _____

4. _____

5. _____

YOUR MONEY CHARACTER

Understanding your 'money character' will help you channel the appropriate methods to manage your money better. Your spending and saving decisions are influenced by physiology as well as psychology, but the good news is that you can modify unhealthy money habits and improve your financial health. It may, however, require a lot of work and discipline over time to accomplish this. Warren Buffett repeatedly quotes Samuel Johnson: 'The chains of habit are too light to be felt until they are too heavy to be broken.' Unhealthy money habits should be replaced with good ones, and this can be done at any time or age. Your money mindset plays a key part in your road to financial success, so it is worth taking time to get it in order first. Have a look and decide which one describes you best. Likewise, identify which character you might like to be.

SAVER	
Lives for the future	Finds it hard to spend frivolously
Thinks long term	
Seeks for money to grow	Tends to be risk-averse
Tends to be goal-orientated	Loves security
Has control of finances	Saves at every opportunity
Enjoys budgeting	

SPEVER (bit of both)	
Likes nice things but doesn't like to spend	Enjoys budgeting with minimal effort
Thinks both long and short term	Accepts risk occasionally
	Saves as and when
Enjoys spending and saving	Enjoys security and freedom
Is goal-orientated but can be impulsive	Needs encouragement to keep control of finances

SPENDER	
Lives for the moment	Impulsive
Thinks short term	Dislikes budgeting
Enjoys spending money	Not a savings lover
Boosts self-esteem by spending	Tends to be a risk-taker
Avoids financial responsibility	Not scared of losing money

- What is your money character?

- What determines this money character?

- What money character would you like to be?

- What traits do you need to adopt to achieve this?

'Money is either a good or bad influence, according to the character of the person who possesses it.'
—NAPOLEON HILL

SWOT ANALYSIS

What **strengths** do you have to help you achieve your goals? What **weaknesses** are standing in the way? How can you maximise the **opportunities** available and what **threats** can prevent you from achieving your goal?

Strengths
- Things that are going well
- Good financial qualities
- Financial knowledge
- Financial assets
- Financially organised

Weaknesses
- Lack of financial confidence
- Lack of financial knowledge
- Fear of finance
- Poor money habits
- Competing with others

SWOT

Opportunities
- Saving regularly
- Spending less
- Reading this book
- Seeking financial knowledge
- Surrounding myself with positive people

Threats
- Poor money mindset
- Negative influential friends/family
- Window shopping (online too)
- Failing to keep up with finances
- Failing to take responsibility

STRENGTHS	WEAKNESSES
•	•
•	•
•	•
•	•
•	•
•	•

OPPORTUNITIES	THREATS
•	•
•	•
•	•
•	•
•	•
•	•

CHAPTER SUMMARY

List three things you are proud you have accomplished after reading this chapter.

1.

2.

3.

Now list three things you will look forward to doing differently after reading this chapter.

1.

2.

3.

What one thing in this chapter inspired you to change the way you think and feel?

Mind Over Money: signs and signals

Here are five signals to help you stay **on track** and five signs to prevent you from falling **off track**.

ON TRACK if you	OFF TRACK if you
Set short-term goals	Have negative feelings towards money
Make your goals visible – use a vision board	Don't make sacrifices to achieve goals
Separate goals into sections	Identify your financial weaknesses
Have and keep a positive money mindset	Don't set priorities
Understand your money character	Overlook opportunities to improve your money mindset

You have arrived at the final stop on your Mind Over Money journey. Remember to take all the knowledge you have gained with you on your next journey.

CHAPTER 3

BUDGETING – TRACK YOUR MONEY LIKE A PRO

> 'A budget is telling your money where
> to go instead of wondering where it went.'
> —DAVE RAMSEY

- Do you find yourself running out of money at the end of each month?
- Do you find it challenging to keep track of your spending?
- Do you struggle to keep to a committed regular saving amount?
- Do you have a budget tracker that's just not working for you?

If you're nodding energetically right now, this book could turn out to be your new best friend, providing straightforward, easy-to-implement strategies to make budgeting a walk in the park!

Budgeting is the foundation of all financial planning and effective money management. If you put one in place at the start of your financial journey, you're already halfway to achieving a more secure financial future. Breaking down the income you receive, identifying your outgoings and highlighting what's left allows you to reduce unnecessary expenses, save more and prevent your funds from spiralling out of control.

When exploring budgeting, you must be open and truthful

about your money and spending, no matter how big or small. There's no need to be ashamed of your finances, and there's little point in not being honest with yourself! It is the simplest way of staying comfortably on top of your finances all year round.

THE BENEFITS OF BUDGETING:

- Controls your money instead of it controlling you
- Increases disposable income
- Helps you save more
- Curbs poor spending habits
- Helps you reduce and clear debts
- Builds financial security
- Helps you achieve and improve financial wellbeing

With so much to gain, can you afford not to budget? You don't need to earn lots of money to cut back on unnecessary expenses and you can never be too bountiful to budget. Take charge of your finances now, and you will be surprised how financially successful you can be over time. This chapter will help you with all the steps you need to transform the way you manage your money.

HOW DO YOU FEEL ABOUT YOUR FINANCES?

Which emoji would you use to best describe how you are feeling about your finances right now? Likewise, think about what emoji you would use to describe how you felt about your finances five years ago and how you plan to feel about your finances in the next five years. Whatever it is, don't worry, there is still time to get things sorted and get to where you want to go, and I will be guiding you through every step of the way. So, you're not alone!

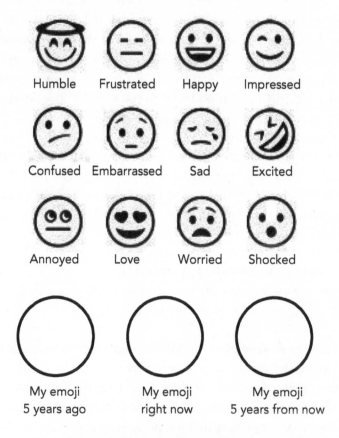

Humble   Frustrated   Happy   Impressed

Confused   Embarrassed   Sad   Excited

Annoyed   Love   Worried   Shocked

My emoji
5 years ago

My emoji
right now

My emoji
5 years from now

TRACKING YOUR INCOME

Understanding your income is critical when budgeting and planning. There are various types of income, and if you're lucky, they might come from more than one source. Aiming for multiple income streams can be a crucial element to achieving financial freedom. This section will provide insight into ways you can understand your income, reduce your tax and accelerate your income potential from various avenues.

Managing employed income

While I have you on a high, let's start with the most regular type of income. You guessed it, the income used to maintain a standard of living is usually from employed or self-employed roles, often referred to as the primary source of income. The income from employment is easy to track as it's normally a similar amount each month.

In contrast, other employed income may vary, such as contracting, which can be tricky to track; but it is essential you do, even if you feel it's not worth budgeting. When budgeting, it is important to use your net income, or the income you receive after tax and other deductions such as National Insurance, pensions and employer saving schemes. So, if you have a gross income (before tax) of £30,000 and a net income (after tax) of £24,000 you should use £24,000 for budgeting, as the remainder belongs to the taxman.

THE PERKS OF BEING AN EMPLOYEE

As an employee, there are bound to be some perks up for grabs that you should take advantage of, such as:

- **Share save scheme** – this allows employees to save towards buying shares in a tax-efficient way. You can save up to £500 per month, normally for three to five years. At the end of the savings period, you have the opportunity to buy shares. The major benefit is that the lump sum you build, as well as interest and any bonus, is tax-free (income tax and National Insurance), although you may be subject to capital gains tax upon sale if you don't invest in an ISA.
- **Salary sacrifice** – an option available to employees who give up some of their salary in exchange for employer benefits, which may include childcare costs, a company car or additional pension contributions. The major benefit is that you will pay less tax and National Insurance, due to reduced earnings.
- **Company car or package** – if you're an employee or an executive, you may be offered or receive a company car or car allowance. A company car can be great if you spend lots of time commuting; it also means you don't have to worry about an additional car cost. Alternatively, you may receive a

car allowance, which offers more flexibility, as the money you receive can be used to purchase a new set of wheels or pay its running costs.

- **Company benefits** – such as dental plans, healthcare, gym memberships, death in service, sick pay and other subsidised benefits.

It's worth speaking with your employer to explore income perks available to you to help you reduce tax.

Managing self-employed income

If you are self-employed, you are likely to have an irregular income and, depending on the type of business; it will vary between steady and shaky. You may have a seasonal business where your income peaks in some parts of the year, but dips during slower periods. In such cases, budgeting can seem complicated and make you want to give up. If you are lucky enough to have income peaks throughout the year, ideally, you should set aside 20% of your net average monthly income to cover shortfall months. For example, if you have worked out an average monthly income of £3,000 during peak months, you should set aside £600 (20%). This way, you will have a more stable income throughout the year rather than a roller coaster revenue. If you are new in business, you can use projections for your budgets, but you will need to update this when you start earning real money. The most important thing is to continue budgeting, regardless of the irregularity.

AVERAGING IRREGULAR INCOME

Self-employed incomes are assessed annually, so there's no surprise many fail to budget monthly. Complicated as it may seem, it is not impossible. An easy way to get an average monthly figure is to take the total income received over a three-, six- or twelve-month period – preferably the latter as the more income history, the better. Next, deduct the tax you are likely to pay based on your tax bracket. If you are not sure, 20% is a useful guide for most self-employed individuals. Then you simply divide the net figure by the number of months, to give an average monthly income figure. It may not precisely represent the income you receive each month, but it will provide an excellent guide to allow you to budget and keep track of your finances.

Example: Amy earned £15,000 over the last six months; however, the income for each month varied. She wishes to average her income to help her budget better monthly.

CRITERIA	AMOUNT
Gross income (6 months)	£15,000
Minus tax (20%)	£3,000
Net income (6 months)	£12,000
Average net monthly income	£2,000

THE PERKS OF BEING SELF-EMPLOYED

1. **You're in control** Owning your own business provides you with full control over every aspect of your company, including who you work with, the environment you work in, your work schedule and your creativity, which allows you to build a business that works for you.

2. **Outsource to others** Being self-employed doesn't mean that you have to do everything yourself. If there are aspects of your business you don't enjoy or that fall beyond your skill set or comfort level, you have the option of delegating or ditching them.

3. **Earnings potential** Unlike traditional employment, where your income is regulated by a set hourly wage or an annual salary, there is no limit on how much you can make at any given time. You may not be guaranteed an immediate profit but putting in the effort and making informed and strategic business decisions can help you achieve your desired earnings.

4. **Claiming some of your costs as expenses** Although self-employed sole traders pay income tax at the same rate as employees, the additional benefit is that you are only taxed

on your profits, rather than overall income. This is because you can claim expenses and allowances to reduce your income and tax. For example, you can claim expenses on car mileage or travel for work. You may also be able to claim work from home tax relief and receive relief on office equipment such as a laptop, desk and chair. You should check with an accountant to ensure you are clear on what you can legally claim for your business.

ADDITIONAL PERKS – FOR LIMITED COMPANIES ONLY

If you are a limited company (separate entity) and you decide to consider the following, it too can have advantageous tax and contingency benefits for your business.

- **Relevant Life** This is a tax-efficient life insurance specifically for business owners, in particular directors of companies (limited liability, partnerships, charity). It is similar to a death in service benefit for employees, only it can offer much more cover. As a director, you have control over the amount of cover you require, but as a general guide, it is normally based on the business value, so the amount of cover can vary greatly.
- **Business Income Protection** A plan designed to financially protect the business if the director (owner) suffers an accident or illness and is unable to run the business. You can set a suitable income that will allow the business to operate if you are unable to, or hire someone else to do your job (if possible). Therefore, it is normally based on the average monthly or annual income the business generates. These plans will also allow you to factor in additional cover to account for pension and National Insurance contributions, which is beneficial to ensure your retirement plans don't halt with your income. You can arrange cover to end on the date you plan to cease trading or to coincide with your retirement age.

- **Pension** As a business owner, you are solely responsible for ensuring you have an adequate pension, which means you may have to work twice as hard. The advantage is, you have the opportunity to choose a more lucrative investment option and contribute as much as you wish (within guidelines), so don't sell yourself short.

The greatest advantage of the above limited company perks is that they are recognised as business expenses by HMRC, which means you can protect yourself, your family and your business, or build a pot for retirement while reducing tax – it's a no-brainer! Check with your accountant to ensure any insurances or pensions deducted from the business are wholly and exclusively for tax purposes. You can also take out adequate protection and a pension as a self-employed sole trader; however, they will not be classed as a business expense and will be treated the same as personal contributions (see page 217).

Creating multiple income streams

A passive income (or side hustle) is any income you receive with no or minimal effort, often referred to as the income you earn while sleeping. There is no denying the work or money involved to achieve this type of income, but once accomplished, it will provide the financial freedom you need to do the things you enjoy, relief from financial stress, and the flexibility to live and work anywhere in the world. Most would agree it's well worth the sweat. Multiple income streams will help build financial stability and financial freedom, something you simply can't refuse. Here are a few types you can consider:

- **Rental income** Income received from renting out a property, commonly derived from a buy to let property (see page 116) or from renting a room.
- **Dividends** Income earned from the profits of a limited company or investment shares.

- **Royalties** Income derived from owning intellectual property such as copyrights, patents and trademarks – usually concerning music or literature. So, if you produce a song or write a book and someone else uses your material to make money, you get paid.
- **Interest income** Income earned from cash savings in the bank or loans.
- **Online income** This is an extremely popular source of income with various ways to gain access to extra cash, ranging from dropshipping to creating an online course, publishing an e-book or becoming an online influencer or YouTube sensation. It will inevitably involve your time and dedication, but if you are successful online, you could be rolling in money in no time.
- **Affiliate marketing** This is the practice of partnering with a company (becoming their affiliate) to receive a commission on a product. This income is generated based on generating traffic or sales for the partnered company's products or services. This method of generating income works best with blogs, websites, social media and even company products. It may take a while to get going, but the passive income will surely be worth the pursuit.
- **Peer-to-peer lending** This is the practice of loaning money to borrowers who typically don't qualify for traditional loans. It is a great alternative to saving your money in a bank account and can pay off if the interest charged is favourable. As the lender, you can choose the borrowers and spread your investment amount out to mitigate your risk. The best way to start P2P lending is to source a website with multiple types of loans with a range of competitive rates. As attractive as rates may seem, you must be aware your money is exposed to the risk of borrowers defaulting.
- **Business** You may have a passion that requires little effort to bring in additional income. Go for it!

To achieve financial freedom, multiple income streams are vital. The world is shifting at an incredible pace, and multiple incomes are becoming the norm. It is up to you to take firm control of the income you receive, and it all starts with your money mindset, planning and the ability to drive your destiny.

 FOR A PERSONAL VIEW: Complete the personal income planner (see pages 273–4)

Income increase (turn up!)

- Ever thought you should be paid more for what you do?
- Ever questioned the real reason you get out of bed every day?
- Ever wondered why you get paid?

We all work for different reasons, whether it be for love, satisfaction, to stay active or, for the majority of us, because we know that if we don't work, we don't get paid. Whether you're working to make ends meet or for a brighter future, wouldn't it be great if your income didn't stop at your salary and you had an unlimited cap – allowing you to achieve all you desire?

But first, you must ask yourself: what truly matters to you? Does the idea of giving back and adding value to people's lives melt your heart, and you wonder why you're stuck behind a desk most of the day? Alternatively, are you career-driven, but find yourself spending more time with the family than you anticipated? Accelerating your income starts with setting priorities. You must decide: is money the bottom line or do your values and beliefs take centre stage? Ask yourself: what income do you truly deserve, regardless of whether it's your employer, your clients or your customers who pay you? What values do you provide that make them want to part ways with their money? List your top three!

The income I deserve is:

Three reasons why:

1. --

2. --

3. --

In an ideal world, you want your income to continually increase. If you feel you are not earning enough, take action, request an increase or up your business prices – because you deserve it! Don't wait for a performance review at work, or for clients to just hand you more money, as this may never happen. You should, however, only take action if you can genuinely demonstrate that you are providing more value to your company or customers. Remember, value is everything, so invest in yourself – whether it's taking time out to acquire a new skill, study for additional qualifications, attend workshops or even read this book! Becoming financially successful is not about how much you earn, but how you invest it!

Mind the income gap

According to the Office for National Statistics, income generally rises with age, peaking between 40 and 49 and often declining after age 50. However, this can differ depending on your profession. For example, most sports professionals have income peaks between the ages of 18 and 25. In contrast, the income of medical professionals tends to peak in later years. Regardless of your profession, you want to take advantage of the years during which your income peaks, aiming to save more than you spend to soften the blow in trough months. If your income gap may be short-lived, you will need to be vigorous with your financial planning. For example, a boxer who may retire in their thirties will need to maximise retirement pots, make long-term investments, and perhaps learn a new skill to help maintain their lifestyle post-career.

> *'If you understood residual income, you would walk through a brick wall to get it.'*
> —ART JONAK

Controlling your income during changing circumstances

Whether you're starting a new job, career or business, it can be an exciting time, especially if there's a pay increase. However, the thought of greater responsibility and changes to your finances can be a nerve-racking experience. Whether your salary is increasing or decreasing, career changes are significant life events that can stress you and your finances. Before you go ahead and throw the towel in, you need to plan. You want a clear picture of what your new income will look like and will need to update your Budget Buddy (see page 281) to ensure it all coordinates. Depending on your latest pay, you may need to make adjustments. For example, if you're taking a pay cut, you will want to reduce your expenditure to ensure things remain affordable for you.

If your pay increases, this doesn't mean your expenses have to follow suit. Try to keep your costs as they are and avoid falling into the trap of 'earn more spend more'. You want to allow yourself the benefit of having a higher disposable income left over each month. How great would it feel, knowing you can have a more significant impact on your future financially? To guarantee you remain on track with your finances during a career change, you should consider the following:

- **Review your tax** If your tax has changed, due to an increase or decrease in your income, review your overall finances. If you have the opportunity, ensure you maximise all allowances and tax reliefs aligned with your tax band, so you can enjoy the benefits without gratuitous amounts going to tax.
- **Review your pension contributions** You may be lucky to have had a recent promotion or a surge in your business. If this is the case, you should consider contributing more to your pension. The major benefit of doing so is you can reduce the extra tax that will come your way, encourage employers to contribute more and work towards a worthy pension in retirement. If you want to build a laudable lifestyle in retirement, you must put the work in; it won't happen if you save just the bare minimum.

On the other hand, if your income has taken a plunge, review your budget to establish an affordable amount. Look at the worst-case scenario, take a break and start again when your circumstances iron out.

TRACKING YOUR EXPENDITURE

Charles A. Jaffe famously said: 'It's not your salary that makes you rich, it's your spending habits.' Understanding your outgoings is vital when budgeting and planning. The expenses list can be endless, and it's easy to lose track of your money. Controlling what goes out will help you avoid unnecessary spending, make better use of your money, and help you enjoy more in life. This section will provide insight into ways you can reduce and maintain your expenses, which fall into two broad categories:

ESSENTIAL EXPENSES These maintain your standards of living and include things like rent, mortgage, food and utility bills. These are usually mandatory and likely to be a fixed or similar amount each month, although they may be subject to change annually. You may have little flexibility over costs and increases in expenses such as rent or council tax, but you do have the advantage of reviewing some essential expenses such as your utility bills or your mortgage when deals come to an end. Take the opportunity to compare the market to secure better deals and save money. Once these payments are set, it's generally at least a year or longer before they can be changed, so make sure you agree on an amount that works for you and your budget. Essential expenses will typically account for a significant proportion of your overall monthly spend. It is important to keep in mind that the more you spend on essentials, the less you will have left to enjoy and save, so aim to keep these expenses low where possible. Ideally, these expenses should account for no more than 50% of your overall net monthly income. In figures, if your total net monthly income is £2,000, your essential expenses should not exceed £1,000.

ENJOYABLE EXPENSES Also known as discretionary spending, fund the things you enjoy, such as hobbies, sport, eating out, shopping, socialising – the list goes on. It also includes all those impulsive purchases that fail to make your budget list. Depending on the mood of the month, these expenditures can fluctuate significantly. Regular changes to your monthly spending make budgeting even harder. Why give yourself a hard time when it is not necessary? You have the upper hand with discretionary expenses; they're flexible, which means you have full control and can change the way you spend at any time. Fun as it may be to go out to fancy restaurants and travel to exotic parts of the world, you must set a limit. Otherwise, you run the risk of losing control of your finances. Your discretionary spending should account for no more than 30% of your overall net monthly income. In figures, if your net monthly income is £2,000, you should spend no more than £600 per month on the things you enjoy. If you are serious about where your financial future is heading, you should limit this to 20%. Think of it as a small sacrifice for a future greater gain. It's a balance: you don't want to cut out the YOLO (you only live once) moments, but at the same time, you don't want them to harness your financial stability. Once you've identified where your money is going, you should have a good indication of your spending habits (good and bad!). Too much flexibility is risky to anyone on the road to financial freedom, so take the steering wheel to control your financial journey.

 FOR A PERSONAL VIEW: Complete the personal expenses planner (see page 275)

Rich money can't fix poor spending habits.

MAKING USE OF THE LEFTOVERS You guessed it: the remaining 20% of your net income should go towards saving and investing in your future. Aim to maximise the following if financial freedom is your destination point.

- Saving
- Investments
- Pensions
- Property

 FOR A PERSONAL VIEW: Complete your budget outcome (see page 279)

50/20/30 Rule

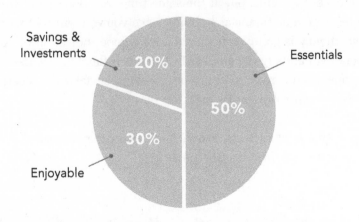

Where is your money going?

Ever wondered how your money disappears so easily each month? Well, here's a few ways to help you identify where your money is going. This simple step will help you take better control of your money so you can direct where you want it to go. Below is an example of some of the common areas we spend.

NOW IT'S YOUR TURN!

Be honest and think of the top eight areas where you spend most each month. You can view your last three months' bank statements to get a clear picture.

Now you know where your money is going, make a list of what you would like this wheel to look like next year.

1. _____

2. _____

3. _____

4. _____

5. _____

6. _____

7. _____

8. _____

HEY BIG SPENDER

- What tempts you to splash out?
- What drives you to purchase items that make you later feel guilty?
- What causes you to say yes to a night out when your only source of cash is a credit card?

In an ideal world, you should earn more than you spend. All too often, this isn't the way it goes! It's tempting to think that the more you make, the more you'll save. The truth is more likely to be that the more you earn, the more you spend. Various factors influence this. It may be rising living costs, social media influences, the availability of fast payments, or your money mindset. Any one of these powerful influences can trigger a button that causes you to spend more. Recognising your triggers is the easiest way to control poor spending habits. So, how can you keep control of your finances and still enjoy life? Yes, you've got to 'put a cap on it', and that means limiting your expenditures.

EX YOUR EXPENSES

Do you need to part ways with some of your expenses? Are you overspending on things such as socialising, holidays or on other people? You may feel like you're living your best life, but you can't live your best life broke. So, do yourself a favour and set a suitable amount for each of your expenses and stick to it. For example, if you only want to spend £200 a month on food but you exceed this each month, the excess has got to go, which may mean you opt for homemade dinners as opposed to takeaways. It may feel like the odd twenty pounds here and there, but it all adds up. Try this with all your discretionary spending, and you may be surprised how much you can save by cutting down some of those non-essential expenses. If you find you regularly exceed your monthly budget, make drastic changes to reduce your spending, to avoid throwing your hard-earned money down the drain. The right balance between pleasure and stability will prevent future financial pain.

TAKE A LOOK AT THE FOLLOWING EXAMPLE:

Alex has £800 set aside for disposable income but wants to buy a home and needs to save for a deposit. He still wants to continue doing the things he enjoys but requires more room for saving. Therefore, he decided on doing the following:

- Socialising once a week instead of twice.
- Avoiding the extra side orders on takeaway and restaurant nights.
- Reducing clothes shopping and comparing prices online before buying.
- Downgrading his luxury gym membership for a basic one.

CRITERIA	CURRENT SPEND	REDUCED BY	SAVINGS
Socialising	£300	£170	£130
Eating out	£150	£100	£50
Clothes	£250	£150	£100
Gym	£50	£30	£20
TOTAL	£750	£450	£300p/m

You can see with just small adjustments huge savings can be made. What can you cut back on to achieve similar results?

'It's not your salary that makes you rich, it's your spending habits!'

—CHARLES A. JAFFE

20 Easy Ways to Reduce Your Spending

Eating out at restaurants	⟶	Order a takeaway
Overspending online	⟶	Set a card spending limit
Going to the cinema	⟶	Catching up on Netflix
Commuting costs	⟶	Working from home
Work lunch costs	⟶	Making lunch at home
Social nights out	⟶	Social nights in
Too many debts	⟶	Cutting up credit cards
Frequently using overdraft	⟶	Reducing overdraft limit
Excessive utility bills	⟶	Switching deals
Enjoying eating out	⟶	Signing up for loyalty cards
High monthly expenses	⟶	Cancel unwanted direct debits.
High mobile phone bill	⟶	Review upgrade opportunities
Always pay full price for items	⟶	Learn to barter (negotiate)
Always spending more than expected	⟶	Plan expenses in advance
Enjoy supermarket shopping	⟶	Get a reward spending card
Buying electrical/tech goods	⟶	Using price match sites
Love discounts	⟶	Don't get duped into overspending
Love buying clothes	⟶	Sell unwanted clothes for cash
Enjoy decorating	⟶	Recycle furniture in your home
Enjoy drinking/smoking	⟶	Try weekly no drink/smoke days

THE RISE AND FALL OF YOUR PURCHASES

It is worth understanding the value of items you consume. Do you spend your money on things that will depreciate or appreciate over time? For instance, a brand-new car will automatically start to lose value from the moment you drive out of the showroom. You may then be lumbered with a hefty monthly payment if not bought outright, only to see no great value at the end. In contrast, a house purchase is likely to start appreciating from the day you move in. Despite still being lumbered with a monthly payment, there is a higher value at the end. Spending money on what we like rather than what we need is a natural human phenomenon. By reorganising your thinking, you might find your buying frequency reduces, and you start to focus less on things that devalue and more on things that add value to your future.

APPRECIATING ASSETS: Appreciating assets are things that retain value and have the potential to appreciate in value over time. However, appreciating assets can also decline in price and lose value over time (like stocks and shares), depending on economic factors and supply and demand. Appreciating assets are great to buy or invest in for wealth-building.

DEPRECIATING ASSETS: Depreciating assets are things that will generally reduce in value over their expected useful life. Some assets will depreciate faster than others, such as cars (particularly brand-new), phones and clothes. However, some depreciating assets will retain value, such as vintage cars and high-ticket or sought-after electronics such as record players. Over time, the depreciation of an asset can make building wealth difficult. Here is a (non-exhaustive) list of a few appreciating and depreciating assets:

Appreciating Purchases	Depreciating Purchases
Property	Cars
Shares	Computers
Government bonds	Computer games
Oil	Phones
Gold, silver & copper	Furniture
Fine wine	Clothes & shoes
Art	Jewellery
Land	Beauty products

* Assets such as shares, bonds and property carry risk, and the value of your investment can rise or fall in line with market performance, meaning you could get back less than invested.

* Supply and demand can influence appreciating and depreciating assets, affecting the value.

MIND THE EXPENSES GAP

Like income, your expenditure is likely to rise and fall, with the highest peak averaging between the ages of 30 and 49 – primarily due to higher mortgage and rent costs, family expenses and our desire to enjoy life. Thankfully, from age 50 onwards, your expenditure should start to decrease as the likelihood is your mortgage will have reduced, children grown, and your lifestyle may not be as extravagant. Reviewing your budget at different stages of your life will give you continuous control of your money. However, regardless of age, you have the power to reduce your spending at any time.

> 'A budget will tell us what we can afford,
> but it doesn't keep us from buying it.'
> —WILLIAM FEATHER

Did You Know?

These figures from the Office for National Statistics are based on how much the average Brit spends on the following each year.

Shopping £2,340   Coffee £600

Eating Out £800

Socialising £3,230   Cigarettes £1,540   Alcohol £800

Perhaps the most striking thing about looking into your finances is the sudden realisation of just how costly your spending habits are. Here's an example I like to use with my clients: how much money do you spend a week on items you don't track?

If you're a coffee lover like me, then you'll know that for some reason coffee made for you by a barista tastes a lot better than coffee you can get at home or in the office. But you'll also know that a medium cup of coffee at Costa is around £2.95. So, picking up a cup every day on the way to work will cost you £20.65 a week (seven days), £89.48 a month (average) and £1,073.80 a year! That's a holiday you're drinking, and it doesn't stop there. If you calculate all your micro-spending habits, I'm certain that you'll find even more ways to save money.

Are you overspending (online or offline)

Most people today are addicted to the internet, and with everything just a click of a mouse away, it's easy to overspend. According to UK Online Mobile & Tablet Retailing (2019–2024) report, over 16 billion is spent online, with expectations to increase to £33.2 billion by 2024. That's over £3.9 million spent per hour . . . shocking!

Many Brits live pay cheque to pay cheque, just making enough to make ends meet, let alone saving. Sometimes, it's because their income is too low to cover necessities. But in many situations, we don't save enough because we spend too much.

Figuring out how to reduce your spending isn't as easy as it sounds, as you may not even realise where you're overspending, and it may be hard to break poor money habits. However, there are many ways to reduce your expenses to dedicate more money to your goals and avoid unnecessary spending that doesn't improve your life or long-term financial situation.

MY TOP 10 WAYS TO REDUCE SPENDING

1. Track your spending

If you're not sure where your money is going, you may end up spending hundreds of pounds a month without even realising it. But if you track your spending, you're more likely to consider purchases more carefully. Tracking your spending for at least three months is typically the first step to effective budgeting because it gives you an early indication of where you need to cut spending. It's also a good idea to track spending on an ongoing basis if you're trying to take control of your money.

Write everything down in a notebook, create a spreadsheet, use an app or make use of the expenditure breakdown on page 278 to give you more consideration and mindfulness before spending.

2. Make a budget

Living on a budget may not seem like fun, but if you're having trouble getting your spending under control, using a budget to limit it is a good place to start. There are a few different budgeting approaches, so you should certainly find one that works for you. If you don't want to go through the process of making a detailed budget that accounts for every pound and penny, you could use a simplified approach such as the 50-30-20 rule.

If you are really struggling to get your money under control, you need to give every pound a job and don't even let one pound escape. That means making a detailed budget specifying how much you will spend (fixed and variable) and how much you will save. If you allocate a budget for your enjoyable expenses, you are more likely to avoid overspending and maximise your savings.

3. Avoid using credit cards

Avoiding credit cards is critical when trying to get your spending under control. Credit cards can give you false hope, making you believe you have enough money to spend, even when you don't. However, you don't want to get rid of your cards entirely, as they can be a great way to develop and maintain a good credit history. It also makes sense to use credit cards for large purchases – as long as you pay off the balance straight away.

It's worth making credit cards inconvenient or difficult to access, so they aren't too much of a temptation, which means you need to get them out of the purse or wallet and put them away somewhere where it's hard to reach. Also, avoid saving your payment details on websites, as this just makes it too easy to unconsciously spend. Trust me: go to settings on your phone or computer and remove all your payment history. It works wonders!

4. Install a 48-hour rule for purchases

A good way to make sure you aren't excessively spending is to force yourself to delay before buying things. When you instigate a 48-hour rule, you stop to think for a couple of days to make sure that what you are buying is really what you need and not some fancy want that you will regret soon after. It's effective not only because it makes it more likely you'll end up only buying things you really want and need, but also because you can use that time to research to ensure you get the best price for your money.

Waiting for 48 hours should also be the minimum; the more you spend, the longer you should wait. For example, 48 hours works great for items below £100; anything up to £500 should be left in the basket for five days, and for any items over £500 you should wait at least a week.

5. Have no-spend days

One of the best ways to cut spending is simply deciding that you aren't going to spend at all. Of course, you can't do this for ever, but you can aim for some no-spend days each month, or if you're really committed, a no-spend day each week. I had a client who managed to save money for her first home by adopting a no-spend Monday principle. Imagine what changes you can make by adopting similar principles.

When you have a no-spend day, you commit to buying nothing other than absolute essentials, such as food or basic living supplies. You could also challenge yourself to see how many no-spend days you can have during each month or how long you can keep up your weekly no-spend days – perhaps compete with your spouse or friend to see who can save the most.

No-spend days not only save you money, but they can help adjust your mindset over the long term. It can help you break your spending habits and develop more creative ideas to meet your needs, rather than just buying new things all the time.

6. Make use of discounts and offers

While cutting spending often focuses on eliminating purchases, there are still some things you have to buy. However, the trick is to save money while doing so. When making purchases, your goal should be to ensure they cost as little as possible. To do that, always try to make use of offers and discounts where possible.

Here are a few ways you can get a discount online:

- First-time purchases on websites
- Social media giveaways
- Selected products
- Buy one get one free or half price

7. Unsubscribe from temping emails

Signing up for email offers from your favourite store may seem smart, especially if you get discounts or special offers mailed to you. But the reality is that promotional offers make you want to buy more. You may see a must-have item or special offer in your mailbox and decide it's too good to pass up, and you end up spending money you wouldn't have. Avoid this temptation.

8. Shop with a list (always!)

A useful way to avoid impulse purchases is to make a list of items you need to buy and then stick to it. A shopping list is common when popping to your local supermarket, but it's even more important and effective when you shop online. Not only do you have the checkout temptations, but you also have pop-up ads with targeted items you love and can't resist. If you're shopping online to buy a pair of shoes and a new coat for work, write it down and don't be swayed by other things you see along the way.

If you are aware of big upcoming purchases, keep an eye open online to ensure you buy items when they go on sale.

9. Avoid shopping when you're hungry

You're probably aware that shopping at the supermarket on an empty stomach means you load the trolley with lots of impulse items. Well, a similar thing happens when you shop online.

Researchers found that a department store shopper who was hungry spent as much as 60% more on non-food products than shoppers who weren't starving. There are evolutionary reasons why you tend to acquire things when you're hungry, so avoid online shopping on an empty stomach.

10. Control emotional spending

Emotional spending occurs when you buy something you don't need or even really want, resulting from feeling stressed-out, bored, under-appreciated, incompetent, unhappy, or indeed any other emotions. In fact, we even spend a lot when we're happy. For instance, what did you buy yourself the last time you got a promotion, passed a test or hit a milestone age?

There's nothing wrong with buying yourself nice things from time to time, as long as you can afford them and your finances are in order. If you're spending more than you'd like to on non-essentials or are struggling to manage your money, pay the bills or pay down your debts, curbing your emotional spending can be an important tool to learn. While avoiding emotional spending indefinitely is probably an unrealistic goal for most people, you should avoid it wherever possible to decrease the damage to your finances.

BUDGET BUDDY

Now you've broken down your income and expenditure, it's time to put it all together to get an accurate picture of your overall finances. Budgeting is about finding a simple system that works for you and setting regular intervals where you check that things are still on track. You can use a Budget Buddy to get the most out of your monthly budget. It also includes a monthly sacrifice that will help you to curb poor spending habits and save more. What can you cut back each month – is it avoiding the morning stop at the coffee shop, sticking to your list at the supermarket, or merely avoiding those irresistible online temptations? You should have at least one sacrifice each month for the benefit of your savings. If you need a bit of encouragement, get a friend or relative involved to cheer you on when you do well or kick you up the bum when you don't! Keep this routine up for at least a year and see how your budgeting and overall finances improve. Use the budget buddy on page 281 to see how friendly your budget looks.

FOR A PERSONAL VIEW: Complete your own personal Budget Buddy planner (see page 281)

> *Budgeting isn't about limiting yourself – it's about making the things that excite you possible.*

Budgeting and banking

Having the right bank account to help with budgeting is vital. It's worthwhile looking into accounts that automatically arrange your finances. Many banks offer budgeting and money management tools that track and show you where your money is going. If you want to maintain control of your spending, you should have at least two separate accounts; one for your essentials and another for your discretionary expenses. Some banks will have integrated systems that allow you to separate your money pots without the hassle of having different banks.

ESSENTIAL BANKING

You should arrange for essential expenses to come from your main current account, which will enable you to set up automated direct debits for most bills. The benefit of setting up direct debits is that your bills get paid on time, which helps build good credit. You may also save money with some companies by setting one up, so it is a win-win scenario. It helps if you have all direct debits collected on the same day, to keep finances simple. Ideally, a day or two after your pay date to ensure there's enough money to cover them. This will avoid you missing any payments, which can adversely affect your credit, and prevent you from spending the money before the bills are due.

DISCRETIONARY BANKING

For discretionary spending, you can set up a separate current account, which can be with a different provider or the same if they allow. It is also worth setting up various accounts to suit multiple enjoyable expenses, such as a luxury pot for lavish spending or a holiday pot for your vacations. You can fund this account each month with a set standing order from your main account, although the date of the standing order should always be set *after* your essential outgoings! The advantage of having a separate account for flexible spending is you can enjoy all the money without feeling guilty. However, once the money runs out, that is it. You must wait for your next pay day before starting the clock again and avoid dipping into other cash accounts. If you can adopt and maintain these practices, the force of habit will keep you in control of your finances, leading to a far more positive attitude towards your future.

Remember, a bank or an app can only do so much to help with your budgeting; you're in the driving seat. The longer you budget, the more benefits you will see, so don't give up.

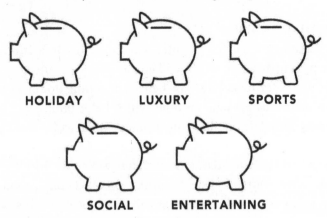

HOLIDAY   LUXURY   SPORTS

SOCIAL   ENTERTAINING

You see, budgeting can be applied in many ways to have a positive impact throughout your life and carry you through changing circumstances. Money will never be your enemy when budgeting is your best friend. Aim to keep your spending at similar levels and try to avoid increasing your spending with your income. Ideally, you should spend less than you earn. It's not how much you earn, but how much you spend, that makes the financial difference; so stick to your limits. The money you have left over after spending should go towards saving or investing in your future.

Take responsibility and ownership of your budgeting as you will only have yourself to blame if things go financially wrong. You have the power to change the way you budget and manage your finances and achieve optimal results. Budgeting will increase your chances of achieving financial growth and success and can be fun if you set methods and routines that work for you.

By continually reviewing your budgets, you will ensure you maximise your full potential. Once you've mastered all we've talked about in this chapter, you will have paved the way to your road to financial freedom – the rest is simple.

CHAPTER SUMMARY

List three things you are proud you have accomplished after reading this chapter.

1.

2.

3.

Now list three things you will look forward to doing differently after reading this chapter.

1.

2.

3.

What one thing in this chapter inspired you to change the way you think and feel?

Budgeting: signs and signals

Here are five signals to help you stay **on track** and five signs to prevent you falling **off track**.

ON TRACK if you	OFF TRACK if you
Track spending – keep all receipts	Spend more than you earn
Set up direct debits – a day after pay day	Splash out before saving
Set an annual budget	Operate all expenses from one account
Explore opportunities for additional income	Give up on budgeting too early
Set priorities and make sacrifices	Overlook the small things that add up

You have arrived at the final stop on your Budgeting journey. Remember to take all the knowledge you have gained with you on your next journey.

PART 2

MONEY MAPPING

You don't need much to start taking control of your finances. The secret is that anyone can achieve financial freedom and it starts by planning – whether its saving, investing or buying your first home.

CHAPTER 4

THE SAVINGS JOURNEY

> *'Save money and money will save you.'*
> —PROVERB

THE PURPOSE OF SAVING

- To fund short-, medium- and long-term goals
- To have protection in unforeseen times
- To keep up with living costs

People save for all sorts of different reasons, such as a car, a holiday, a house, for security or retirement. Whatever the reason, it's essential to have the right mindset in place. Savings are the foundation of financial security and will be there for you when you need it most. If you're a lover of spending, you may genuinely not see the point of saving, but the glaring truth is that none of us know what the future holds. Savings provide a safety net, a cushion on which to land in the event of unexpected and unforeseen circumstances. They allow you to remain financially stable should you lose your job, or if you're facing a sudden hike in living prices, and give you time and peace of mind while you put other plans in place.

If you can commit to saving, it will help you achieve your short-, medium- and long-term goals, whether that's starting a new business, buying a home, or funding education. The big question is, can anyone afford *not* to save? It's a myth that saving is difficult, impossible or will pause the party. This chapter will guide you through effective ways to save so that you can continue with the things you enjoy, while still contributing towards your future. It will also help you avoid opening yourself to risk, such as financial debt and imbalance. So, don't procrastinate; start right away.

I was 16 years old and working in the bank as a cashier. Mr Cavendish, one of our customers, came into the bank to do his usual top-up on his savings passbook – he enjoyed seeing what interest he had incurred on his six-figure saving each month. However, on this occasion something was wrong; he was not happy and complained about a discrepancy of two pence. At first, I thought he was joking as I couldn't understand why two pence would be of such importance to a wealthy man like Mr Cavendish; after all, it was money even the less fortunate would throw down the drain. However, I could tell from the stern expression on his face that he was serious as he waited until the issue was rectified, and the two pence was added back to his account. He must have seen the baffled look on my face as he leaned over to me, looking smug, and said, 'If you ever want to be rich in life, never take a penny for granted.' From that day on, I took saving seriously.

START YOUR SAVINGS JOURNEY

When planning a journey, you need to map out where you want to go and how you will get there, and the same principles apply to your savings journey. As you think about your future, you want to identify your goals to make saving much more meaningful and fun. Each goal you set should have a price tag. You may be looking to save £5,000 for a car or £30,000 for a deposit on a property. By setting a price for your goal, you can quickly work out how long it will realistically take you to achieve it. It may only take twelve months to save for a car, whereas five years might be needed to gather a property deposit.

First, you have to begin, which may mean cutting back on a few things. The amount you start with doesn't really matter; it's better to start small than not start at all, so don't get discouraged. It may take you longer to achieve your goal, but you will have put yourself on the right road. And let's face it, there's no more superior feeling than the smugness of knowing you're doing the sensible thing. If you have the flexibility, you should put away at least 20% of your net monthly income, and if you are serious about saving, opt for 30% – which should form part of your essential expenses. Yes, that's right, save before splashing out. If your surplus income is slim and you're unable to save 20%, you can reduce it to a more affordable amount. Aim to save at least half of whatever you have left over, so, if you have £200 disposable income, you should aim to save at least £100. If you're still not convinced, look deeper into your flexible expenses and see what spending can be reduced. Instead of using your money to buy things you don't need or can do without, you can put it towards your next holiday or buying your first home sooner. Sacrificing some of your luxuries for your goals is a prominent part of a successful savings plan.

 FOR A PERSONAL VIEW: Complete the savings tracker on page 284 to help you get started

5 STEPS TO BUILDING A SUCCESSFUL SAVINGS PLAN

Once you understand the importance of saving, and how to do it successfully, you should be geared up to start. Before you dive in, let's explore the steps of saving, to make sure you put your money in the right place to work just as hard as you do.

1. **Saving Purpose**. Think about the reason why you are saving or want to save; it may be growth or future stability. Your saving will have more meaning if there is an underlying purpose.

2. **Saving Frequency**. Think about whether you will save a lump sum or a regular amount; this may depend on whether you are cash- or income-rich.

3. **Saving Term**. Aim to set a timeframe, as in how long you will save. Will it be in the short or long term? Once the timeframe is set, try your best to remain committed to your plan.

4. **Savings Goal**. A goal will specifically set out what you want your savings to help you achieve, whether that's saving for your child's university fees or to fund your annual holiday. Your goal will help you choose the right savings account. For example, if you are saving for your first property and need an account that will pay bonuses to help you build a deposit quicker, you may therefore consider a Lifetime ISA (see page 87).

5. **Savings Pots**. Once you have identified what your savings goal is it's time to set up a savings pot. Separating your savings into various pots will help you remain focused and committed. Here are a few pots to get you started.

HOLIDAY CAR SOCIAL

WEDDING FAMILY STUDY

The most important savings account: the emergency fund
The first type of savings everyone needs is an emergency fund, one you will rely on in unforeseen circumstances such as loss of income, a death in the family or a world crisis. Ideally, your emergency funds should be at least three to six months of your monthly income. If you earn £2,000 (net) per month, you should have £6,000–£12,000 saved to supplement your income in unexpected periods. If you are starting from scratch, here is some perspective: to build a £3,000 emergency fund in one year, you need to save £250 a month or £125 a month for two years. If you are a high earner or have irregular income, you may prefer to have six months' worth of emergency funds to provide more peace of mind. You need not be overly concerned about achieving the best interest rate on your emergency fund account. The main priority is that money is readily accessible. Once you have built up your emergency fund, just forget about it. It is the only way you can guarantee there will be a financial cushion to rely on when you need it most.

Saving for an emergency fund doesn't have to be difficult. Here is a simple guide:

1. Add up all your expenses
Essentials:	£1,500
Enjoyable:	£400
Savings:	£100
Total:	**£2,000**

2. Multiply your total expenses by 3 (months)
Total: £2,000 x 3 = £6,000

3. Set an emergency fund timeframe
In one year	£6,000 , 12 = £500 per month
In two years	£6,000 , 24 = £250 per month
In three years	£6,000 , 36 = £166.67 per month
In four years	£6,000 , 48 = £125 per month
In five years	£6,000 , 60 = £100 per month

FINDING THE RIGHT HOME
FOR YOUR MONEY

Current accounts, cash in your pocket or cash stuffed under the mattress – none of these should be an option. You are merely selling yourself short, as these methods will not pay you anything back. And even if your religious beliefs prevent you from earning interest, it's still not a good idea to keep money under the mattress for the simple reason it's far too accessible – and might not be under the mattress for long. Here are some more sensible options.

Deposit account (easy-access)
- Minimum amount: £1
- Maximum amount: Unlimited
- Tax: Taxable
- Age: From birth
- Risk: No risk to capital (Protected by FCSC)
- Access: Instant
- Term: Short-term savings

A deposit account is excellent for short-term goals between one and twelve months. You may have plans to buy a new car, fund education or travel abroad within a year. These accounts are straight-forward, and most you can start with as little as £1. There are no caps on the money you can put in, which is excellent if you have large amounts to save. You will receive minimal interest, but the benefit is that you have easy access to your money. Interest rates are variable, so do keep an eye out for any sudden interest rate changes. A deposit account is not ideal for long-term savings unless it is used to hold emergency funds, which should be held for life.

Premium bonds
- Minimum amount: £25
- Maximum amount: £50,000
- Tax: Tax-free

- Age: From age 16
- Risk: No risk to capital (government-backed)
- Access: Instant
- Term: Short–medium-term savings

Premium bonds have been popular since 1861, meaning they have survived two world wars. They offer tax-free savings and are backed by the government. You can access your money at any time with no restrictions. But the most attractive thing about premium bonds is the winning element. You have the opportunity to win up to £1 million with a mere £25 deposit. So, literally speaking, you could become a millionaire overnight. Instead of the interest that most savings offer, premium bonds enter you into a monthly prize draw where you can invest anywhere between £25,000 and 50,000. Before you start dreaming of all the things you can do with a million pounds, you should understand the downsides too. Sorry to break it to you but the chances of you winning a million are quite slim. For the majority of investors, the average win is £25 over two years, which means if you invest £5,000 over two years, your return would be a minuscule 0.5% (per year). Therefore, it's fair to say the winnings over the long term may not be as satisfying. But if you like a bit of a gamble while staying safe, this could be the account for you.

Regular savings account
- Minimum amount: £1
- Maximum amount: £250 per month
- Tax: Taxable
- Age: From age 16
- Risk: No risk to capital (protected by FCSC)
- Access: Instant
- Term: Short-term savings

If you want to get into the habit of saving regular saving accounts are a great option. You can save a fixed amount each month while earning a higher interest rate than general saving accounts, especially when they are linked to the same bank as your current account. Due to higher interest rates, there are often restrictions on how much you can put in and take out. These accounts are excellent for short-term targeted goals such as buying a car, going on holiday, or treating yourself to something nice.

Notice account

- Minimum amount: £1–£1,000 (depending on provider)
- Maximum amount: Up to £1,000,000 (may vary)
- Tax: Taxable
- Age: From age 16
- Risk: No risk to capital
- Access: Notice required
- Term: Short–medium-term savings

These offer flexible access, however; as the name implies, you are required to give notice for any withdrawals. The notice period generally ranges between 30 and 180 days. Notice accounts pay higher interest if you keep to the rules and avoid withdrawals without sufficient notice. They are ideal for short-term goals between one to two years. You can use this type of savings account as a holding home for your money before you commit to other purposes. These accounts will reward you more the longer you save and may pay you bonuses. However, there may be penalties if you wish to withdraw your funds before a set term. Therefore, it is vital to understand how committed you are to saving before considering these types of accounts.

Fixed-rate bonds

- Minimum amount: From £1,000–£10,000
- Maximum amount: Up to £1,00,000 (may vary)
- Tax: Taxable
- Age: From age 7
- Risk: No risk to capital

- Access: Notice required
- Term: Short–medium-term savings

Fixed-rate bonds are suited to medium- to long-term savings, and you can take out bonds from six months to five years. Fixed-rate bonds offer a guaranteed rate of interest over a set period. Throughout this period, there are withdrawal restrictions, and you cannot access your money unless the bond is broken (closed). The minimum input amount is generally higher than other savings accounts, but there is no maximum limit. After opening, you cannot contribute further, but you can add more when the bond matures. They offer higher interest rates compared to other savings accounts due to more onerous restrictions and are attractive for those who don't need access to capital but prefer a risk-free environment.

Individual savings account (ISA)

First introduced in 1999, ISAs are tax-efficient accounts (free from income and capital gains tax but may be subject to inheritance tax), which can be held in a cash saving, investments, or peer-to-peer lending account. They can be used to meet short-, medium- or long-term goals such as buying a property, saving for a family or planning for retirement. All ISAs have a set limit known as the ISA allowance and can only be held in sole names. If you or your spouse or civil partner dies, you can inherit their ISA allowance and vice versa in addition to the normal ISA allowance. The tax-free amount can be added to the value of the ISA upon death, or the value of the ISA when closed. To be sure of the terms of an ISA, you should contact your ISA provider for details. The list below gives further details of all current ISAs.

CASH ISA

Minimum opening amount: £1
Maximum amount: £20,000 per tax year
Age: From age 16
Access: Instant*

A cash ISA is the same as a deposit account with a shiny wrapper from the government that allows you to save tax-free. You can set up a cash ISA as a deposit, notice or fixed-interest account so pick the one that best suits your savings plan. Cash ISAs are instant-access accounts and may, therefore, offer low interest rates.

HELP TO BUY ISA (HISA)

Minimum amount: up to £200 pcm
Maximum amount: £200 pcm
  (total maximum amount of £12,000)
Age: From age 16
Access: On buying the first property

Introduced in March 2015 to help first-time buyers save for a deposit on their first home. HISA is no longer available to new savers and was replaced by the Lifetime ISA in November 2019. However, if you opened a HISA before this date, you can continue to contribute until 2030. The maximum you can contribute is £200 per month, which will be matched with a £50 bonus each month from the government (you need to save a minimum of £1,600 in order to qualify for a bonus). In total if you save the maximum of £12,000 and include the maximum bonus of £3,000 you would end up with a deposit of £15,000, which provides an excellent stepping stone to buying your first home. Also, if you are saving with a partner, together you can achieve a total of £30,000 towards your first home.

LIFETIME ISA (LISA)

Minimum amount: £1

Maximum amount: £4,000 per tax year

Age: From 18 to 40 (to open, but you can continue
   to contribute up to the age of 50)

Access: When buying your first home, at age 60 or above, or if
            terminally ill with 12 months to live. (Withdrawals for
            any other reason will be subject to a penalty charge.)

Launched in April 2017 (to replace the HISA), the LISA can either help you either to buy your first home (with a property value of £450,000 or less) or to retire. You can save up to £4,000 each year and receive a 25% bonus from the government each month. This would result in a £1,000 bonus for every £4,000 saved per year, which may be appealing if you need further assistance buying your first home or retiring. You must keep the account open for a minimum of 12 months before withdrawing funds to avoid a penalty.

INNOVATIVE FINANCE ISA

Minimum amount: £100 (may vary)

Maximum amount: £20,000 per tax year

Age: From age 18

Access: Set out in the terms and conditions of the account.

A peer-to-peer lending type of ISA is where you lend money to individuals and businesses like a lender. In return, they pay you back a fixed interest over a set period, and it's all tax-free. Without the bank acting as the middleman, you have a direct relationship with the borrower, making saving that bit more meaningful and exciting. However, with this comes more risk, since borrowers can default and fail to pay you back, although most peer-to-peer lenders vet borrowers to make it safer for you, so the chances of this happening are quite slim. But to be on the safe side you should check the track record of the platform you are investing in and what protection they provide for lenders.

STOCKS AND SHARES ISA

Minimum amount: £1–£100 (different providers may have varying minimum amounts)
Maximum amount: £20,000 (per tax year)
Age: From age 18
Access: Any time, although depending on investment
  liquidity it may take longer to gain access to your money.

Stocks and shares ISAs can be invested directly into shares or a combination of bonds, property, equities and other assets. Investments can be a lump sum or regular amount. The significant advantage is you can achieve compounded growth and diversify your money with no tax to pay on the income or gains. Unlike cash ISAs, stocks and shares ISAs carry risk and therefore you should only invest in areas that fit within your risk appetite. But if you are happy taking some risk on your money, stocks and shares ISAs have the potential to provide greater returns over the long term. Your stocks and shares ISA is likely to include investment charges, so do ensure you are familiar with the costs involved and how they may affect your growth.

JUNIOR ISA (JISA)

Minimum opening amount: £1–£100 (may vary)
Maximum amount: £9,000 (per tax year)
Age: 0–18
Access: Restricted (accessible only on the child's 18th birthday).

There are two types of Junior ISAs: a cash Junior ISA, where you will pay no tax on the interest of the cash you save, and a Stocks and Shares Junior ISA, where your cash is invested, and the capital growth or dividends you receive is tax-free.

  Your child can have both types of Junior ISA as long as the annual allowance is not exceeded. You cannot have a Junior ISA and a Child Trust Fund (CTF), the long-term tax-free savings account launched in 2005 (but no longer available to new investors). However, you can transfer the funds of a CTF into a JISA. Parents or guardians with parental responsibility can open a JISA, but the money belongs to the child. When the child reaches 16, they can have full control of the account (JISA cash only) but cannot access the money until 18.

* The following savings figures, including minimum and maximum amounts, tax-efficient status, qualifying criteria and age range, are subject to future changes, and the amounts and ages may differ depending on the provider.

* The savings figures provided are for general guidance, and you should seek financial advice for personal recommendations.

* Stocks & Shares ISAs carry risk; the value of your money can go up and down, and you could get back less than you initially invested. Innovated Finance ISAs carry borrowers default risk.

* If your ISA is 'flexible', you can take out cash then put it back in during the same tax year without reducing your current year's allowance. Your provider can tell you if your ISA is flexible.

** You can have a combination of ISAs in a given tax year; however, you cannot exceed the annual allowance limit. Stocks and shares ISAs and Innovative Finance ISAs only allow you to have one in a given tax year.

*** You can transfer your ISA from one provider to another at any time or to a different type of ISA or to the same type of ISA. For example, you can transfer the value of your cash ISA to a stocks and shares ISA or vice versa.

THE STEPS OF SAVINGS

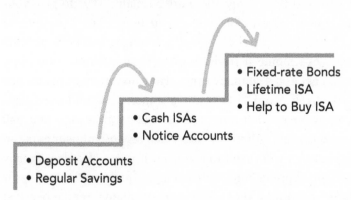

• Fixed-rate Bonds
• Lifetime ISA
• Help to Buy ISA

• Cash ISAs
• Notice Accounts

• Deposit Accounts
• Regular Savings

These savings stages are the way most people build up their savings over time. Although this may be different for some individuals, this guides you through the general attitudes of most savers in different groups.

The first step on the savings ladder usually involves cash. Cash is the only asset that most people between school age and post-education will own. After that, it is common for individuals to want more of a balance between savings and growth, and therefore look for accounts with a better return, such as ISAs and notice accounts. Further down the line, you may naturally be more interested in long-term products due to income flexibility and being more serious about your future. It is at this point you may want to consider exploring investing.

> *It's not about how much money you make,
> it's how much you save that makes
> the difference.*

HOW TO SAVE MONEY WITHOUT EARNING MORE

If you can find the energy, there are so many ways to give your savings a new lease of life and get to that desired place for a better financial life. I live and breathe a budget, and I love finding new ways of keeping it fresh, to make saving simpler and more effective. I get asked so many times, 'How do I manage my money more effectively?' and 'How can I save money, when I don't have anything left over each month?' It's really simple, and you will be amazed at what difference little changes and adjustments can make. Trust me: you've got to try! Even if you feel you've already blown it by dipping into your savings, spending beyond your budget or skipping a few credit card payments, remember, just because you made a few mistakes, it doesn't mean you can't try again and have success. Here are five savings tips you can consider:

1. Examine your spending

The COVID-19 pandemic helped many people re-evaluate their spending and has forced us to focus on needs versus wants. During lockdown periods, our socialising, entertainment and many other luxuries were restricted, which gave some the ability to save for the first time or increase their existing savings. With this in mind, take a look at how you managed to reduce costs; instead of waiting for a pandemic, apply this to your everyday routine. Then, use the extra cash to pay off your debt or build up an emergency fund. By doing so, you can instil good habits to prosper in future.

2. Budget for savings

Warren Buffett is often quoted as saying: 'If you want to make saving a priority, take a look at how you budget.' In other words, if you want to start or build savings – or even consider investments – you need to include this in your budget and treat it as an expense. Think of it as a payment towards your future lifestyle. If you are serious about building wealth, you have to do more than save from the leftovers. We achieve what we prioritise. So go ahead and prioritise your savings!

3. Set specific goals

Simply writing down 'I will save more' isn't tangible enough; you need a bit more meat on your goal wishbone if you want to be successful at accomplishing goals. If you want to save more, come up with a number and write it down, preferably using pen and paper. (Research shows that the manual act of writing means that whatever you have written is more likely to remain in your memory, making it easier for you to recall your goals later.) Whatever goal you set should be realistic and measurable. When you're able to measure your objectives, you'll find it much easier to track progress and work towards achieving your goal. So avoid setting too many!

Once your goals are noted, try setting dates in your planner and revisiting them often to check your progress. Alternatively, print out your goals and place them in areas where you might stumble upon them without meaning to. It will give you the continual motivation you need to succeed.

4. Revisit subscriptions and direct debits

It's time to take it down a notch; after all, all these subscriptions add up, and those free trials tend to be unbelievably short. According to YouGov, Brits waste over £800 million on unwanted subscriptions. You may have signed up for some monthly subscription services that you rarely use, so it's time to reassess them and get rid of any you no longer want or need. Start by making a list of all your subscriptions and critically assess whether you're getting the full value out of them. You might find you have multiple subscriptions that offer a similar or the same type of service. By reducing even a few subscriptions, you can save hundreds of pounds every year.

5. Invest time in learning about money

Financial literacy and education are not just for the rich and wealthy; they are for everyone. It's vital we educate ourselves about money as we interact with it in our everyday lives. Being financially literate enables you to make smarter money decisions and helps you build a secure financial future, one that protects your assets, business and loved ones. Financial literacy typically covers financial issues like budgeting, spending, debt, taxes, retirement savings, investing, mortgage management and estate planning. If sufficient time is spent learning about finances and managing money matters, you will reduce financial stress and anxiety.

> *'Just do your best and realise that it is enough. Don't compare yourself to anyone. Be happy to be the wonderful, unique special person that you are.'*
> —SUSAN POLIS SCHUTZ.

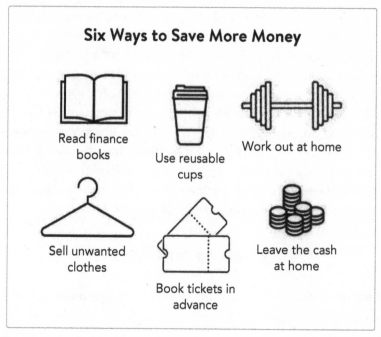

Six Ways to Save More Money

Read finance books

Use reusable cups

Work out at home

Sell unwanted clothes

Book tickets in advance

Leave the cash at home

Can you think of other ways you can save money?

1.

2.

3.

What would you do with the extra cash?

1.

2.

3.

Hopefully, you now understand the importance of savings, and how to choose the right home for you and your money. You should feel confident to start saving or adjust your existing savings accordingly. Online saving platforms have made it much easier for you to make an informed choice but it's important to continually monitor your savings, at least on an annual basis or if your circumstances change. For example, if you have a pay increase or a bonus, you should review your savings plan as this will help you identify opportunities to save more and earn better interest. Likewise, unless the interest on your savings account is fixed it is subject to change, so keep an eye out for any reductions. Remember, savings kept in cash accounts for extended periods may not keep pace with inflation (cost of living), which could impact the value of your savings. So, stick to your savings plan to maintain the purchasing power of your money.

CHAPTER SUMMARY

List three things you are proud you have accomplished after reading this chapter.

1.

2.

3.

Now list three things you will look forward to doing differently after reading this chapter.

1.

2.

3.

What one thing in this chapter inspired you to change the way you think and feel?

Savings: signs and signals

Here are five signals to help you stay **on track** and five warning signs to prevent you falling **off track**.

ON TRACK if you	OFF TRACK if you
Set a savings goal	Save with no purpose
Find the right savings account for your money – one with the best interest	Don't keep sufficient money aside for an emergency
Add saving to your essential expenses	Keep money in savings over the long term
Save regularly without dipping in	Dip into your savings regularly
Separate your savings pots	Don't save at all

You have arrived at the end of the Savings journey. Remember to take all the knowledge you have gained with you on your next journey.

CAN YOU SPOT THE DIFFERENCE?

Employed full-time and earns £100K p.a.	Employed full-time and earns £40K p.a.	Self-employed and earns an average £25K p.a.
Lives at home with parents	Rents with a housemate	Owns her property
Drives a Mercedes worth £60K	Drives a BMW Mini	Does not drive
Loves to eat out at fancy restaurants	Loves to order takeaways	Enjoys cooking at home
Enjoys shopping and buying luxury items	Enjoys shopping and buying bargains online	Not a frequent shopper
Has a pension with work and invests the maximum	Has a pension with work and invests the minimum	Has a personal pension and contributes 3%
Has credit card debt of £3,000	Has credit cards but no debt	Has credit card debt of £500
Has a disposable income of £1,500 pcm	Has a disposable income of £500 pcm	Has disposable income of £200 pcm
Does not save each month	Saves £400 each month	Saves £100 each month
Has total savings of £5,000	Has total savings of £48,000	Has total savings of £5,000

As you can see, there are multiple differences. Overall, it shows it's not about how much you earn but what you choose to do with the money, the way you use it, spend it and save it. We can all make some commitment to saving if we truly want to, no matter how small. So, do away with the myths that you need to earn lots of money to save and build wealth. If you don't have the right mindset how much you earn is irrelevant, as shown in the examples above.

'In the long run it's not just about how much money you make that will determine your future prosperity. It's how much of that money you put to work by saving it and investing it.'
—PETER LYNCH

CHAPTER 5

BORROWING – THE GOOD, THE BAD AND THE UGLY

> 'There can be no freedom or beauty in a life
> that depends on debt and borrowing.'
> ——HENRIK IBSEN

What one person may deem a good reason to borrow may not resonate with another; we all have different reasons and priorities. But one thing that remains the same is borrowing can be risky, especially if you are unaware of the consequences. You may wish to borrow for a house, which is the most common and worthwhile type of borrowing. Alternatively, you may want to borrow to expand your business in the hope of a substantial return, which in itself isn't a bad idea. If you decide to borrow to invest in increasing assets, this may not be as risky and can pay off. However, if you're borrowing to keep up with social trends, buy luxury items or head off on holiday, that does need careful thought. There's little point borrowing to buy items that will go out of fashion because with the added interest, you could end up paying them twice over.

Credit boosts credit

In terms of your credit rating, well-managed debt can help boost your credit. Conversely, it can have adverse effects, and in the worst-case scenario cause you to lose control of your finances. To avoid this, you should always borrow within your affordable means.

Create a borrowing plan

Before you consider borrowing, you should have a specific reason. Is it to buy a house, expand a business or buy the latest designer handbag? A borrowing plan will establish the purpose for borrowing and help you work out what you can pay back and how long the debt will take to clear. It will also help you establish what you can afford; anything additional will only leave you high and dry. If paying back is not your thing, take my advice and steer clear of borrowing altogether.

TYPES OF BORROWING

If you are looking to borrow, there are many options you can consider, but choosing the right one can sometimes be tricky. This section will give you all you need to know to stay on the right side of borrowing.

> *'A bank is a place that will lend you money*
> *if you can prove you don't need it.'*
> —BOB HOPE

Credit cards

Credit cards are suitable for short-term borrowing and are generally easily accessible and offered by most banks, stores and even supermarkets. You'll likely be offered one when you open a current account. The amount and interest offered will usually depend on your income, money management history and credit scoring. However, most credit cards charge high interest, often double-digit figures. Credit cards are great for large purchases such as electrical items and flights as they offer purchasing protection. They are also useful for short-term cash flow but beware, they are highly addictive, and it's not hard to spend more than you bargained for.

FINDING THE RIGHT CREDIT CARD

Finding the right credit card can be confusing with so many options on the market. Before you go shopping for a credit card, aim to identify the right one for you, your goals and your spending habits. The following shows some of the options available:

CARD TYPE	DESCRIPTION
0% interest	A card with 0% interest means there is no interest to pay throughout the introductory period, which ranges from 3 to 24 months. They are generally offered to loyal customers or those with good credit. The significant advantage is you can clear your debts more quickly, as you are not paying interest. Providers will likely lure you in with 0% interest on balance transfers to encourage you to transfer other credit card debt. These credit cards are almost too good to be true. Well, there is a catch: most providers will charge you a fee on balance transfers, which typically range between 1% and 3% (anything above can be quite excessive), while some may express the fee as a monetary amount. Therefore, it's worth calculating the costs to see if it's worthwhile. You can do this by adding the fee to your transfer amount and dividing it by the number of months in the introductory period to work out the total you'll pay back over the period. With no monthly payments for a set period, you can easily forget you still have a debt to pay. Once the initial period ends, the interest is likely to revert to a much higher rate. So, you should consider how the money will be paid back and spend sensibly.

CARD TYPE	DESCRIPTION
Reward card	Reward cards offer the opportunity to help save hundreds on your everyday spending. Sounds tempting; however, most reward cards require you to pay off the balance each month to avoid interest or receive the best rewards. If you enjoy travelling, this could be the perfect credit card for you as you can earn points on every flight or holiday you book, and if you build up enough points you can get free trips. However, you should check the value of points and charges before committing. Aim to look for a card that offers high reward points with low or no annual fees.
Cashback	These cards are pretty straightforward: for every pound you spend, you get a percentage as cashback. They are great for shopping and general daily use, and if used enough, you could save hundreds on your weekly shop. However, make sure you read the small print as some cards will require a minimum spend to be eligible or charge high interest if the balance is not paid in full each month.
Student credit card	A student credit card is for those in higher education. You must be 18 or over and have a student bank account to be eligible. You may also receive rewards when you spend, including cashback and loyalty points. However, they generally offer low limits and will often charge high interest rates.
Classic credit card	Classic credit cards are vanilla with no sprinkles. You use them to purchase goods and services but beware every tap is likely to cost you in interest. You should aim to pay these cards in full before your monthly billing date.

* The following borrowing figures, including interest rates, balance transfer fees, qualifying criteria, and terms and conditions, are subject to future

changes, and the interest rates and balance transfer fees may differ depending on the lender.

* The borrowing information provided is for general guidance, and you should explore the lenders full terms and conditions before deciding.

Buy now pay later

This is an increasingly popular payment option offered by Klarna, PayPal and other online retailers for online purchases such as clothes, shoes and even furniture. It offers interest-free payment periods and no credit scoring, which may sound attractive, but taking advantage of such offers could be an easy way to slide into debt or incur hidden fees you are unaware of. So, ask yourself, can you pay now? Do you really want (or need) to pay later? Save yourself time and trouble and leave it in the basket if you can't afford it.

Bank overdrafts

An overdraft acts as a short-term financial cushion for unexpected day-to-day expenses. It is an amount the bank will apply to your current account if you go below zero. It can be particularly useful for those who are self-employed or who do not have a regular income that arrives on the same day each month; it can help you avoid defaulting on regular payments, which will cause bank charges and leave a dent in your credit rating. The agreed over-draft amount you are offered will depend on your income, account management and credit scoring and can range from hundreds to thousands. It is not suitable for long-term borrowing as they usually charge daily interest or monthly charges, which can quickly rack up. Therefore, you should avoid being overly dependent on your overdraft.

Personal loans

Personal loans offer straightforward borrowing for your personal needs, such as a new car or debt consolidation. There are various types of personal loans, so you should research the market to find the right one. Personal loans are more suited for long-term borrowing as they offer competitive interest rates, making monthly payments more affordable. Your credit scoring will be the ultimate deciding factor in the interest rate charged, the amount borrowed and acceptance. One of the major advantages is a fixed monthly payment, which makes it easier to budget and keep on track. Unlike a credit card, you can select the term of borrowing, ranging between one and seven years, although you may wish to pay it off before the end of the term. You can generally borrow up to £25,000 and will have the option to increase or decrease borrowing, subject to approval. The table below shows other types of loans available.

LOAN TYPE	DESCRIPTION
Student loan	If you have been to or are currently attending university, you're likely to have been exposed to the word 'debt'. A university education is one of the most significant debts people take on in their teens. Student loan debt will keep building while you study and takes a lifetime to clear after graduating. However, it's not all doom and gloom. One benefit of student loans is they don't show up on your credit file and will not affect your ability to borrow elsewhere. However, they do attract interest if your income is over the threshold, which increases the more you earn. Therefore, you may consider making overpayments to reduce your loan. There's no penalty if you make extra repayments, but they are not refundable, so it should only be considered if you don't need the money. Review your student loan regularly; if your income increases, you may be required to contribute more. Set a career goal and take advantage of the interest-free periods, to remove debt more quickly.

LOAN TYPE	DESCRIPTION
Hire purchase loan	This is often a way to finance buying a new car – usually one you can't afford! You pay a lump sum deposit, and the remainder of the car value will be collected as fixed monthly payments over one to five years. The loan is secured against the car, which means you don't own the car outright until the loan is settled. Interest rates for hire purchase loans are usually higher than personal loans, although the acceptance criteria are more lenient.
Family/friend loan	You might be worried to ask a family member or friend for help, unsure of the response or what they might think, even if you are a frequent family/friend borrower. The truth is borrowing money from a family member or friend is no different to borrowing from the bank. However, with this type of loan, your loyalty is your bond, and it's one you don't want to break. Failing to pay back money to family or friends will not result in bailiffs or county court judgments but it can ruin your relationship and could lead to nasty disputes. Avoid this at all costs – keep your end of the bargain.
Payday loan	You may need money in an emergency, and with no emergency fund savings, you may find yourself opting for a payday loan. They offer quick access to cash in exchange for hefty interest rates. It would be best if you didn't touch them with a barge pole, or at least put them right at the very bottom of the borrowing possibilities. Unlike other personal loans, these loans are short-term with payback options over days or several weeks. However, if not paid back on time, you can end up paying a fortune in charges, sometimes double or triple the cost of the original loan. You only need look at the fine print of most payday loan agreements to run a mile.

WHEN DEBT GETS UGLY

Bad debt is when high interest rates are applied, or when someone consistently invests in depreciating assets such as clothes and cars, which can lead swiftly to financial difficulties. Here is an example:

Melissa buys a car that costs £20,000. She put down a £5,000 deposit and borrowed the remaining £15,000 through a hire purchase loan. She had fairly good credit and secured a loan at 10.9% over 36 months with monthly repayments of £490 per month*. After three years, Melissa paid back £17,653 (an additional £2,653 in interest). She then decides to sell her car and upgrade to a newer model costing £30,000. However, her car has dropped in value and is only worth a woeful £11,000 – almost half the original amount. She sells the car for £9,000 and uses this as a deposit for her new car, only to repeat the process.

*This calculation is based on Auto Trader, who accepts no responsibility for any loss or miscalculations that may arise. All calculations made in this calculation are to be used as guidelines only.

So, there is no doubt this sort of debt means you lose out at a high cost and, therefore, should be avoided if you want to maintain financial stability.

Good vs bad

In the early days of the social audio app Clubhouse, I shared a virtual stage with business entrepreneur and bestselling author John Lee, discussing this very topic. It is important that you do away with the myth that all debt is bad. A simple rule to apply is that a good debt will put or keep money in your pocket, while bad debt will take money from your pocket. Here is a non-exhaustive list (in no particular order):

GOOD DEBT	BAD DEBT
Mortgages	Bridging loans
0% credit cards	High-interest credit cards
Borrowing from friends and family	Payday loans
	High-interest loans
Low-interest loans	Hire purchase
Student loans	Overdrafts
Government loans	Arrears
Business loans	

Not all debt is bad

A good debt that is well controlled helps you achieve a healthy credit rating, which speaks a good word to lenders if you want to obtain a mortgage or loans. On the other hand, if you have no debt at all, there's no means of proving how well you'd manage it if you did and oddly enough, this in itself can harm your credit rating.

Good debt generates little or no interest on borrowings; thus the overall repayment is similar to the amount initially borrowed. However, if stretched over the long term, you end up paying a considerable amount in interest, which should be avoided where possible. Debt is also perceived as beneficial if explicitly used for an investment that will increase in value, such as property or a business.

> *'Good debt is a powerful tool, but bad debt can kill you.'*
> —ROBERT KIYOSAKI

CHAPTER SUMMARY

List three things that you are proud you have accomplished after reading this chapter.

1.

2.

3.

Now list three things you will look forward to doing differently after reading this chapter.

1.

2.

3.

What one thing in this chapter inspired you to change the way you think and feel?

Borrowing: signs and signals

Here are five signals to help you stay **on track** and five signs to prevent you falling **off track**.

ON TRACK IF YOU	OFF TRACK IF YOU
Keep overall debt below 30% of the total credit	Use credit cards when you can't afford it
Are sensible with borrowing	Ignore red flags
Choose the best type of borrowing for your needs	Borrow to buy depreciating assets
Borrow for appreciating assets	Buy now, and don't pay later
Review your borrowing regularly	Allow borrowing to negatively affect your credit score

You have arrived at the end of the Borrowing journey. Remember to take all the knowledge you have gained with you on your next journey.

CHAPTER 6

PROPERTY – NAVIGATE YOUR WAY TO BUYING A PROPERTY

> *'Property is an imperishable asset ever increasing in value. It is the most solid security that human ingenuity has devised.'*
> —RUSSELL SAGE

Buying a property is one of the most significant purchases you will make in your lifetime, so getting it right is crucial. The process can be long, with most of the work required well beforehand, for example, setting a goal, building and maintaining credit, saving for a deposit and familiarising yourself with the process and costs. Buying a home can be daunting, especially if it's your first time. However, this chapter aims to help make the process less painful and more straightforward by guiding you through all the essential steps you need to take before and after buying.

THINGS TO CONSIDER BEFORE YOU BUY

To buy or not to buy?
With property prices continually rising, renting may be your only option. However, let's have a look at some of the positives of buying, as the idea of renting for life or sofa surfing over the long term may not be that appealing. Owning your own home offers the benefits of security, equity and potential growth in your

wealth. The value of a house will appreciate over time, and if you decide to sell, you can earn a profit. Another advantage is creative control over your property. You can make changes to suit your style, paint the walls whatever colour you fancy, or build a studio in the garden with no complaints. Also, you have the option to rent out your property to produce additional income. What's not to love?

Get your credit up

It is essential to maintain a good credit score when considering buying a property. Ultimately this governs the final decision, and just a minor mistake such as a missed payment can cause an application to be declined. And let's face it; no one likes rejection! There are several things you can do to help boost your credit score. Firstly, make sure you have some credit history; ideally, you should have a debit and credit card and manage them well. Make sure you are registered on the electoral roll at your current address. Lenders like to see a three-year history of addresses. Lastly, start paying for utility bills – gas, electric or council tax (mobile phones don't count!) or put your name on one as soon as possible. This will have a significant impact on your overall score. Keep a regular check on your credit; if something doesn't look right, aim to rectify it as soon as possible to avoid leaving a footprint on your file.

Set the date

Set the date in your diary and call it 'Property Purchase Deposit Achieved'. Seeing it in black and white may be the encouragement you need to get you over the final hurdle.

> *Go ahead and set the date – what's to lose?*
> *The date I will buy a property*
>
> . . . .

> *Owning a home is a keystone of wealth . . .*
> *both affluence and emotional security.*

THE PROPERTY PURCHASE PROCESS

The process of buying a property can take the best part of three months, sometimes longer, so you must be aware of all the steps involved, so you don't trip up along the way. This section will explore all you need to know when purchasing a property.

Financing your property purchase

The first step before you start looking for a property is establishing how much you can borrow. The amount a lender will lend heavily depends on your income, typically based on a multiple of four to five times your annual salary. For example, if you earn £30,000, you can generally borrow between £120,000 and £150,000. If you are self-employed, the lender will normally take an average based on the last three years' accounts, although a few will take your latest year of accounts into consideration. However, several factors can affect your affordability, such as your expenditure, debts, deposit and your credit score. It goes without saying that if you have minimal expenses or debts and a good credit rating, you will get the highest borrowing. Can you see why budgeting is so important? You can easily get an idea of how much you can borrow online, but avoid formal applications until you are in a position to buy as it will leave a footprint on your credit file.

 FOR A PERSONAL VIEW: Complete the property savings tracker (see page 285)

Finding your home

Once you know how much you can borrow, you are ready to start your property search. With most properties advertised online, it's easy to compare, filter and search for properties effortlessly. Once you find a few that you really like and that tick the right boxes on your checklist, you will want to arrange a viewing.

Getting a good estate agent on your side always makes property buying more seamless. They often know about potential properties before they go on the open market and can supply other important information. A good estate agent will help you narrow down your selection, assist you with viewings and negotiate the best offers, so when you find one who's good – hang on to them. Look for an agent who has worked for some time in the area of interest. You can get a recommendation or contact them directly, even if they're not advertising a property that interests you.

 FOR A PERSONAL VIEW: Complete the property wish list (see page 286)

Making an offer

You'll know when you find your dream property; you'll feel it in your gut, so don't second-guess yourself. Your checklist is likely to have many ticks, and the property should bring more excitement than nerves. Speak to the estate agent, who will help you make a realistic offer, and then go ahead, hit the button! However, stick with your budget and an offer you feel is right. Consider the condition of the property and any compromises you have to make. If you find a property you like that is not ready for you to move in or is in dire need of a makeover or a structural uplift, you'll need to factor the additional costs into your overall budget or make sure these are reflected in the asking price. You can gauge a fair asking price based on similar properties sold in that area or by purchasing a valuation report; both are great tools for negotiating. Once this has been done, you can start the formal buying process. The final steps to completing your property purchase are the financial and legal requirements, so before you pop the bubbly, be sure to get these in place.

Arrange a survey/valuation report

A property valuation is an inspection that identifies the value of a property. It is required when you take out a mortgage and is normally paid for upfront. It takes into account the location and condition of a property. It helps ensure you are paying an accurate price for the property compared to similar properties sold on the market. Once you are certain of the property you wish to purchase, you can instruct a surveyor to do a house survey. It is the lender of your choice who will recommend the surveyor, so that's one less thing you have to worry about. You have the option of three different types of surveys, which vary in cost due to more thorough checks. It may seem appealing to go for the cheapest option, and in some cases, such as for new builds, this would be more than sufficient, but paying a little extra can help highlight any hidden defects or damage, saving you lots of money in the long run. Here are your survey options:

- **Condition report** – describes the condition of the property, identifies any risks and potential legal issues and highlights any urgent defects – but not in great detail. It's most suitable for new-build and conventional homes in good condition; no advice or valuation is provided in this survey.
- **Homebuyers report** – offers a report that identifies any significant damage or future repairs such as subsidence or damp and other internal or external issues. Suitable for those looking for a broad overview of the property's condition or opportunities to renegotiate the original offer. Ideal for first-time buyers or non-conventional purchases.
- **Full building/structural survey** – provides a more thorough internal and external inspection of the property than the homebuyers report. The surveyor will have a full look at the property, including the types of materials used, the condition

of the roof and the structural integrity. They will often lift floorboards or check behind walls for any issues. Your report will include all aspects of the check and a list of recommendations with concerns about required changes. This report is the most expensive but ideal if you buy a non-standard construction such as a thatched or steel-framed house.

The application

The mortgage application is bound to be one of the most inter-rogating financial experiences you will encounter, so it's worth all the painstaking preparation, even if you have gone through the process before. It can still seem very overwhelming – once you have signed the application and your solicitors exchange contracts, there's no going back; the deal is done.

Here's a list of what you will need to complete a mortgage application:

- ✓ Payslips for the last three months and a P60 (for employees)
- ✓ Audited accounts for the last three years (for self-employed and directors)
- ✓ Proof of dividends (for directors of limited companies)
- ✓ Self-assessment accounts (for self-employed)
- ✓ Bank statements for the last three months (proof of income)
- ✓ Identification i.e. driving licence/passport (proof of name)
- ✓ Utility bill for the last month (proof of address)
- ✓ Up-to-date credit report (for personal use)

TYPES OF BUYERS

Whether you are purchasing for the first time or moving home, your circumstances and requirements will be unique. The lender will offer an array of products and interest rates depending on what type of buyer you are. These are the main types of borrowers.

First-time buyer (FTB)

If you have never owned a property, you are classified as a first-time buyer. There are many government schemes and attractive mortgage incentives specifically targeted to FTBs, which include low fees, free basic valuation, or cashback options. If you are buying your first home, take advantage of the schemes, offers and saving options (HISA or LISA) available to help you along the way. Alternatively, you may have the pleasure of financial support from the 'Bank of Mum and Dad'. If you decide on a government scheme route, explore all your options, and decide on the most suitable.

FIRST-TIME BUYER SCHEMES	
Help to Buy or Equity Loan Scheme	The Help to Buy Scheme is designed to help those with a small deposit. The government offers an equity loan for first-time buyers and for existing homeowners who want to buy a new-build home. If you have a 5% deposit saved, you can borrow an additional 20% of the purchase price, interest-free for the first five years. If you live in London, this increases to 40% of the property price. The scheme is available until 2023. The maximum property price is £600,000 in London (price caps will differ depending on region).
Shared Ownership	Shared ownership is where you buy a share of a property as opposed to purchasing a property outright. For example, you can buy 50% of a property; the remaining 50% will be paid as rent to the landlord (council or housing association). For this reason, you only need to acquire a mortgage for the percentage of the property you own. You can choose to buy a more significant share of the property up to 100% of its value. To be eligible for shared ownership you must have a household income of less than £80,000 (outside London) or £90,000 (inside London). You must be a first-time buyer, a previous homeowner or own an existing shared ownership property requiring you to move.

FIRST-TIME BUYER SCHEMES	
Mates Mortgages	Mates Mortgages has become a growing trend, where borrowers club together to pool resources to form a larger deposit or generate more income for a mortgage. This option is available for up to four borrowers. However, the majority of lenders will only take into account the two borrowers with the highest income. You should consider this type of mortgage carefully as the implications of purchasing with a friend need to be very clearly understood. It can be stressful enough living in harmony with friends, let alone sharing a big financial commitment.

Buy to let (BTL)

A buy to let is a residential mortgage used to buy a property for rental purposes. Unlike residential mortgages, they are assessed on the rental income of the property (usually a minimum of 125% of the monthly mortgage payment). For example, if your monthly mortgage payment is £1,000, you will need a minimum monthly rental income of £1,250. So theoretically speaking, you don't need to be earning a penny to take on a BTL mortgage. However, some lenders will require a minimum income figure.

Right to buy

If you are a council or housing association (HA) tenant, you can or may have the opportunity to buy your home under the right to buy scheme. Right to buy offers huge financial discounts of up to £112,300 (£84,200 outside London), which can be a great stepping stone to get on to the property ladder. You must meet the eligibility criteria, such as having fair credit scoring and the ability to afford the remaining mortgage. It helps if you also have some savings, as some lenders may require you to have a deposit of your own. But if you don't have a deposit, many lenders will still be willing to offer a right to buy mortgage. The remaining mortgage process is very similar to the traditional mortgage route.

Intergenerational mortgage

These mortgages are designed for parents or grandparents who wish to help their children or grandchildren get on the property ladder.

RESIDENTIAL VS BUY TO LET

If you are thinking of buying a property and can't decide between residential or BTL, here are a few pros and cons to help provide clarity.

	RESIDENTIAL	BTL
PROS	Low deposit – as little as 5% Decorate as you wish No income tax No capital gains tax (main residence only) Eligible for residency relief (IHT) Opportunity to rent a room	Mortgage paid by tenants Creates passive income Mortgage assessed on rental income No/minimal income needed to apply Can buy through a company
CONS	Can be considered a liability if not producing growth or income Liable for monthly payments Stricter mortgage acceptance Affordability is based on income Cannot buy through business Renting restrictions may apply	Higher deposit – minimum 25% Additional stamp duty Finding tenants is time-consuming Landlord maintenance costs Tax liability – income, CGT and IHT Landlord legal obligations

MORTGAGE OPTIONS AND AVENUES

Once you have an agreed mortgage it's time to decide on your options.

Choosing the right repayment option

REPAYMENT
A repayment mortgage consists of capital and interest, which will clear the mortgage in full if paid until the end of the term. It is excellent if you are looking to be mortgage-free at the end and is the preferred option for most residential buyers.

INTEREST ONLY
This consists only of interest, which means the capital amount you borrow will remain outstanding at the end of the mortgage term. For example, if you borrowed £300,000 over 25 years, you would still have to repay £300,000 at the end of the term. It may be an attractive option if you are looking for a lower monthly payment or plan on selling the property before the end term. For this reason, it is usually the preferred option for buy to let mortgages because they are self-financed. If buying a residential property, you may consider an interest-only mortgage, but most lenders will require a minimum of 25% deposit and a repayment vehicle such as an investment or a pension to repay the mortgage at the end of the term. However, you must be aware that there is no guarantee that any will meet the target to pay off your mortgage at the end of the term.

MORTGAGE TERM
This is the time you choose to pay back the mortgage. The most common mortgage term is 25 years; however, you can take a term up to 40 years in most cases. The mortgage term should ideally end before your anticipated retirement date. If you choose a term beyond, you will need to prove how you will afford the mortgage in retirement, for example, sufficient income from a pension.

Choosing the right product

There are two broad products you can choose: fixed or variable.

FIXED RATE

A fixed product is a rate you choose at the outset that is fixed for a set term. A fixed rate is typically over 2, 3, 5 or 10 years with some lenders offering lifetime fixed rates. The advantage of a fixed rate product is they are excellent for budgeting. However, the downfall is if the bank reduces the base rate throughout your fixed period, you could end up paying above-market rates.

VARIABLE RATE

A variable or tracker is a rate you choose at the outset that can vary over a set period. Variable rates track the Bank of England Base Rate (BEBR) and therefore are subject to change. There are various variable products to consider, as listed below:

Standard Variable Rate (SVR)/Tracker: The SVR is the rate that your product normally reverts to when your deal comes to an end. You should avoid staying in an SVR for long periods as the interest tends to be extremely high.

Offset: Offsets savings held with the mortgage provider and therefore generally offers a lower rate. These are great if you have no plans for your savings.

Capped: A variable rate with a specific upper limit known as a cap. The interest rate can fluctuate but will not go above the cap.

Collar: A variable rate with a specific lower limit known as collar; it will not fall below this rate but can rise with no limit.

Discount: A variable rate with a set discount off the SVR. For example, if the SVR is 5%, the product may offer a discount of 2%. Therefore, the discount rate would be 3% for a specified period.

THE MORTGAGE COSTS

Buying a home isn't just about saving for a deposit; you will almost always pay more than you initially expected. It is crucial to think about all the other costs so that you know exactly how much you will need to acquire a property. The costs involved will depend heavily on the type of buyer and the property price. These are the other costs you should become familiar with.

Deposit
The percentage of the property price you pay in cash: the higher your deposit, the lower your interest rate and monthly mortgage payment.

Stamp Duty Land Tax (SDLT)
This is tax paid on the purchase of property, land or physical transfer of a property. The tax paid will vary depending on the property price. There are incentives for first-time buyers and extra tax applied to second purchasers. Depending on where you live, SDLT may apply different tax and rules. There are also special rates that apply to purchases such as corporate bodies, shared ownership, purchases that mean you own more than one property and trust purchasing properties. For further details see www.gov.uk.

Valuation and surveyor costs
The cost of a survey can vary depending on the size of the property and purchase price and therefore could be more or less than quoted (see page 122).

Legal fees
Legal fees are paid to the solicitor to deal with the transfer of deeds. They will also conduct searches and release funds. The fees can vary depending on a variety of factors such as property type, area or also the time it takes to process from start to finish. Some solicitors offer fixed costs, which are much easier to budget.

- **Local authority searches** – identify plans and developments surrounding your property.
- **Land registry search** – registers the property in the new owner's name.
- **Environmental searches** – checks for any history of flooding, mining and subsidence.
- **Electronic transfer fee** – the cost of transferring funds on completion.
- **Bankruptcy searches** – checks to ensure the buyer is not bankrupt.
- **Solicitor's fees** – the cost of legal work.

Product/booking fees

This is the amount you pay to secure the most exclusive deals, and the lowest interest rates will come at a higher cost. You need to work out if it is worth paying a higher cost to keep your monthly payments low or whether you are happy to pay higher monthly payments to reduce the upfront costs. The advantage you have is the opportunity to add product fees to the mortgage if you are short on cash or you prefer to keep some back. However, you must be aware that adding the product fee to the loan will mean you pay back more interest in total – you will be surprised how much £1,000 can compound over 25 years.

Broker/adviser fees

Suppose you are unsure how much you can borrow, the best lender to choose and the cheapest products on the market. In that case, a mortgage adviser can help and can also assist with unique requirements, such as mortgages for those with poor credit. They will charge a fee for arranging and advising the mortgage on your behalf, which could be a fixed fee or a percentage of the property price. You should expect to pay more for a mortgage adviser with considerable experience or expertise.

If you feel confident after reading this book, there are online platforms where you can do it yourself, especially if your situation is relatively simple; therefore you dodge paying additional fees. In some ways buying a property is like all 'shopping'; you can suddenly find you've ended up spending much more than you intended. On average, it's a good idea to set an additional £5,000 aside for residential purchases. Make sure you study and compare the market so the decisions you make will be educated ones.

THE COSTS AT A GLANCE			
Cost	Criteria	Residential	Second or Multiple Properties
Deposit	Percentage of the property value	5–10% (5% deposits are common with FTBs but are not always available and will depend on the lender if offered)	25% (BTL only)
Stamp Duty Land Tax (from October 2021)	Up to £125,000	Zero	3%
	£125,000–£250,000	2%	5%
	£250,000–£925,000	5%	8%
	£925,001–£1,500,000	10%	13%
	£1,5000,001+	12%	15%
Valuation fee	Basic valuation	£150–£400 (however, as an incentive some mortgage offers will cover the cost of the valuation, particularly common when conducting a remortgage)	Same

THE COSTS AT A GLANCE			
Cost	Criteria	Residential	Second or Multiple Properties
Survey costs	Condition report	£300–500	Same
	Homebuyers report	£400–£1,000	
	Full building survey	£600–£1,500	
Legal/ conveyancing fees	Local authority searches	£250–£450	Same
	Land registry fee	£200–£300	
	Telegraphic transfer	£20–£30	
	Title deeds	£10	
	Property fraud checks	£30	
Product fees	Booking fee	£99–£250	Same
	Arrangement fee	£0–£1,999	
Broker/adviser costs	Amount	£500–£2,000	Same
	Percentage of the loan	0.5–2%	

* The following mortgage-related figures, including fees, charges, tax and criteria, are subject to future changes, and the interest rates charges may differ depending on the lender.

* The cost information provided is for general guidance, and you should seek mortgage advice for personal recommendations.

OTHER CONSIDERATIONS

Once you get the keys, you may be excited about your new purchase. However, there are a few final steps to contemplate before you celebrate. Buying a home is likely to be your biggest financial commitment, and so you can't afford to skip the things you need to do after purchase. Ideally, you should set an overall buying budget that will also include pre- and post-purchasing costs such as:

* **Removal costs** These will depend on your circumstances, but you should set aside some extra cash. An average cost is £500 and potentially more if you include packing, dismantling and reassembly. If you purchase a buy to let, you may not have removal costs, but you may need to buy white goods such as a washing machine or a fridge to comply with landlord requirements.
* **Maintenance repair and decorating** One of the first things you may consider when moving home is doing up the property to suit your desired taste and style. However, this comes at an extra cost, meaning you should set a budget to avoid going overboard and leaving yourself out of pocket.
* **Personal insurance** You may need to consider this to ensure you are not left with a horrible debt in the event of an unforeseen crisis (see Chapter 9).
* **Buildings and contents insurance** Buildings insurance will cover the rebuild cost of your home in the event of a disaster such as a storm, flood or fire. Buildings insurance is compulsory and your mortgage provider will normally request to see evidence of a policy before exchanging contracts. Contents insurance will cover all the moveable items in your home, such as furniture, jewellery and clothing, in the event of theft, fire or accidental damage. You can also insure your personal possessions that you carry out of the home, such as a watch or a wedding ring – it's not

compulsory, but it's better to be safe than sorry!

- **Council tax** Before moving, it's worth checking the council tax amount on your new home. It will allow you to update your budget, so you have a clear picture of your future expenses. If you are buying alone, you may also be eligible for a single person discount.

Fleeing the nest

Moving out of your family home is a big event, which can make you feel excited and anxious at the same time. You can finally have the freedom you may have been longing for. However, this freedom comes at a price as you will be independently responsible for your finances and bills. It may be the first time you ever pay rent or a mortgage payment, but it certainly won't be the last – so familiarise yourself as early as possible. If you are already in a routine of paying your parents a monthly sum, there shouldn't be too much of a financial shock. It will still take some time to get used to increased expenses, but it will soon settle in. Ideally, you want to set a budget before you flee the nest. Ensure you're financially ready and avoid any unwanted surprises. Think about your income and see what is affordable beforehand. You also want to consider whether you will cook at home or eat out and factor in those costs. If you are on a low budget, you may decide to stay close to your parents – if you're lucky they'll cover your weekend dinners!

If you find the monthly living cost too expensive to manage independently and you have a spare room, you can opt for a flatmate. Sharing housing costs with someone else will certainly lighten the load, but you need to be sure they'll keep their end of the bargain. If you choose to have a flatmate, you should get a legal contract drawn up to protect yourself if they fail to keep up with their financial commitments. Avoid rushing or pressuring yourself to make rash decisions. Take your time to find somewhere you're comfortable with that offers your preferred amenities and fits your budget. Budgeting might not be the most exciting thing to think about when leaving home, but you will surely thank yourself for it later.

PROPERTY ROADBLOCKS

What if I am nowhere near?

With rising property prices and standardised wages, it's no surprise many struggle to get on the property ladder. The average property purchasing age is continually rising and is currently 33, so don't get discouraged if you're still renting or living at home with parents. It's fair to say saving for a deposit may seem a mammoth task – you may feel it's too expensive, and you'll never actually be in the position to buy. But with the right planning, you can get your foot on the property ladder sooner than you think.

How much do I need?

If you're a first-time buyer, you may be wondering how much money you need to get on the property ladder. Generally, you need to save at least 5% (ideally 10%) of the property price you are purchasing. So, if your desired property is £270,000 (average house price in the UK 2021, ONS), you need to save £13,500 (£27,000 for 10%), although if you have the opportunity to save more, you will benefit from a wider choice of lenders and cheaper interest rates. Then there are the other costs involved (see page 122). In short, it is wise to set aside an additional £5,000 buffer to cover all your associated mortgage expenses. Once you know the property you are looking for, you can efficiently work out how much you need to save.

What's my price range?

The price range will depend on how much a lender will let you borrow combined with your deposit. For example, if a lender is willing to lend £150,000 and you have £10,000 saved as a deposit, the maximum property price you can consider is £160,000, unless you are buying through a help to buy scheme (see page 116), which will provide an additional deposit, meaning you have more flexibility with the property price.

Can I buy in time?

You are probably wondering about the best and quickest way of buying a property. It may take a year or five years; what matters is your commitment to securing your property. Have a look at your savings budget and see how much you can realistically afford to allocate towards your deposit each month. Is there any potential to increase your monthly savings? Prioritising is key to achievement; it may mean putting luxuries on hold until you have built up the deposit you need. There's nothing worse than finding a property you love only to see it go because you're not in a position to buy.

What if I can't afford to buy?

What you can afford will depend on your income and financial support. Can you buy alone, or do you need to partner with someone? Should you decide on the latter, you should choose your property partner wisely. Splitting the costs may sound like a good way of saving money. However, if you choose the wrong person, it can be an expensive mistake and a complicated process to undo. Don't be afraid to ask for help from parents, family members or a friend to help you get your foot on the ladder. You must do whatever it takes to get there. If you are still living with your parents, this provides an excellent time to plan and save as much as you can before the real responsibilities kick in. Discuss your options with them as they may be able to provide financial support or if not, certainly the benefit of their own experience. Wherever you are in the property process, you should start a property plan and the sooner, the better.

ARE YOU READY?

Now you have all you need to purchase a property with your eyes wide open, fully equipped with all the necessary information, and should be ready to buy with confidence – which can feel like an outstanding achievement. However, there's no shying away from the work involved in reaching that point, from setting the goal, to the blood, sweat and tears of building a deposit. You will feel genuinely thankful for all the work you put in. Remember to consider all other associated costs, both pre- and post-purchase, and ensure your monthly mortgage payment is affordable as your home could be repossessed if you do not keep up with your monthly payments.

CHAPTER SUMMARY

List three things you are proud you have accomplished after reading this chapter.

1.
_____

2.
_____

3.
_____

Now list three things you will look forward to doing differently after reading this chapter.

1.
_____

2.
_____

3.
_____

What one thing in this chapter inspired you to change the way you think and feel?

Property: signs and signals

Here are five signals to help you stay **on track** and five warning signs to prevent you falling **off track**.

ON TRACK if you	OFF TRACK if you
Open a property savings account (LISA)	Give up on your property goal
Save more than your deposit	Dip into your property savings
Stick to your property plan and wish list	Sign documents without reading them properly – several times
Build and maintain good credit	Don't take advantage of FTB incentives
Compare the market for the best deals	Skip on insurances after purchase

You have arrived at the final stop on the Property journey. Remember to take all the knowledge you have gained with you on your next journey.

WHAT DOES FINANCIAL SUCCESS LOOK LIKE FOR YOU

Circle the things that resonate with what financial success means to you and try drawing some of your own.

FLASHY CAR   CHAMPAGNE   BUYING A HOUSE

MONEY   HOLIDAYS   OWN BUSINESS

PHILANTHROPY   FINE DINING   EDUCATION

SOCIAL STATUS   PARTIES   SHOPPING

Financial success doesn't have to be all fancy stuff.
Insert your own thoughts here.

- -

PART 3

FINANCIAL TRANSITIONS

Throughout your life, you're bound to experience changes that will influence the way you think and feel about money. It may be hitting a milestone age, getting married, getting divorced, or starting a new family. We have a natural ability to adjust and adapt to life's constant changes. However, without the right planning, your finances can easily get left behind or lost in the past, while significant changes in circumstances can derail you and your finances. So how do you stay on track during unexpected chapters in your life – good or bad? How do you get yourself back on your feet financially after being knocked down? Conversely, it might mean remaining humble and modest if your money speeds ahead. Setting a relevant plan to fit around new situations will help you regain and retain control throughout life's changes. Also, it will help balance your money and wellbeing, while preventing a vast amount of stress and anxiety – ultimately keeping you on the road to financial freedom.

CHAPTER 7

MONEY AND MARRIAGE

> *They say love is more important than money, but have you ever tried to pay your bills with a hug?*

Managing and merging your money can be one of the most difficult challenges couples face. It's a transition that should be dealt with delicately. Whether you're married, in a relationship or have a business partner, you want to establish the best way to share money and decide who (if not both of you) will deal with the finances so that everyone is happy. There is no right or wrong way to manage your finances with someone else. You may choose to merge all your accounts into joint names or keep separate accounts. The important part is to set a fair, transparent financial plan that works for you and your partner, so you both know what to expect. Don't put off discussing important financial issues with your partner; state your financial goals and even your financial fears to identify where you both align or disagree entirely. This way, there will be no surprises ahead.

GETTING IT RIGHT FROM THE START

Marriage is a joyous thing, but if the finances are not right, it can bring anguish. No matter how good you are with money, if you marry someone with poor financial habits, it will affect you somehow, some day! So, how do you keep things merry for the benefit of your marriage, your finances and your peace of mind? You may have different beliefs and values and possibly share different experiences and backgrounds with money. Financial differences are one of the main reasons marriages split, so do what you need to get and keep things right – and the sooner, the better.

Communication is key

The first step to get on track with your coupled finances is communication. Most people don't discuss money in the early stages of their relationship, which can cause financial issues in later years. Talking about money will lay a strong foundation and provide the harmonious balance you need. You should discuss everything, including goals, aspirations, assets, debts, values, beliefs – basically, anything that involves money. By doing so, you can see where you agree or disagree; there's no point in lying or holding back as it will only come back to bite you later. Suppose you're not so great at communicating – in that case, you may feel more comfortable downloading a credit report and letting your partner view it and vice versa. You never know how you or your partner's credit may affect the other, so this is vital, especially if you live together. You should have this conversation as early as possible, ideally before the wedding or moving in together. This way, you can prepare yourselves for managing your household finances and decide who will control the financial affairs, if you are not going to manage them jointly. Aim to work together to build a secure financial future and resolve any financial issues you may have, ensuring that you are both heading in the same direction.

Discuss your couple goals

Couple goals go far beyond those couple poolside pics (with all the 'likes') you see on social media. It's more about financially planning together, so you can continue the lifestyle you enjoy together, now and in future. The most divisive thing you can do is secretly set separate goals and expect things to fall into place. Find common ground with your partner and be prepared to compromise. It may be that you both love going on holidays, but only one of you is prepared to save. In such a case, perhaps one of you can take responsibility for the holiday fund while the other covers the daily household expenses. This way, you both get to do the things you enjoy without getting into debt or arguments.

INVESTMENT GOALS

If you have a common purpose you want to achieve over the long term with your partner, it's worth considering joint investments. For example, you may both have plans to move abroad or build a lump sum to buy a property. In this case, you jointly contribute to your goals. The benefit is you can both hold each other accountable to remain committed and focused, and you can achieve your goal in much less time.

RETIREMENT GOALS

Don't wait until you are ready to retire to have these discussions – the earlier the better. You may not be able to have a joint ISA or pension, but that shouldn't stop you from discussing your retirement goals together. Have a look at the following questions and try answering them with your partner.

- Who will earn the most in retirement?
- What age do you both wish to retire?
- What will happen if one of you retires before the other (usually if there is an age gap) and the household income significantly reduces?
- How will income be supplemented if one partner is a low earner?
- What other options are there to provide income in retirement if you have decided not to contribute to pensions?

MATCHING YOUR MONEY CHARACTER

There are few things more thorny than a person who loves to save, partnering with someone who loves to spend. But the relationship can still work if you plan together. If your partner is not good with money, try to keep positive and be supportive as this will help your spouse feel more confident to make a change. If you're the one with poor money management, you should pat yourself on the back for reading this book. You want to discover each other's personalities early on, so you can build a more compatible financial future. Which joint character describes you and your partner?

The spender and the saver

You could be the best saver in the world, but if you meet up with a spender, it could be difficult to curb their love of spending. For spenders and savers to develop a healthy relationship, there has to be some give, and sacrifices have to be made. Either the saver will rub off on the spender or vice versa. To make this relationship last, you must strike a balance and stick to it. It would help if you both commit to limits: it can't be all saving and no enjoyment; likewise, it can't be all spending with no plan for future commitments. If this sounds like you and your partner it won't come as a surprise to learn that you will have a lifestyle clash at some point in your relationship (if you haven't already). You both need to compromise to make it work.

The spender and the spender

For this relationship to last, you both need to be bringing in the cash or rolling in it, as it fits the life of the wealthy. Even if you do happen to have money to splash, it is not the best idea to continually spend. You want to build a future legacy, and that is not achieved through spending alone.

The saver and the saver

Let's say your future together is secured financially. You are both dedicated and believe in your future. It can be a harmonious relationship but make sure you set plans for your savings so you can both enjoy and reap the benefits of your hard work.

THE MONEY MINDSET QUIZ

Once you have established your joint money character, have a go at answering the questions below with your partner, to gain a more in-depth insight into both your financial beliefs and goals. Find out how much you know about your other half!

Make sure you have some snacks to hand; it's about to get interesting. Oh, and don't forget the tissues as there may be some tears (hopefully of joy!). It's just a bit of fun but, in all seriousness, understanding more about each other's money mindset will help you build a better harmonious relationship with each other and with money. This quiz works brilliantly with a bestie too.

1. When you hear the word money, what's the first thing that comes to mind?
2. What did you learn about money growing up?
3. What did you do with your first pay cheque?
4. What is the best thing you have ever bought?
5. Does your star sign play a part in how you handle money?
6. What's your worst financial habit?
7. If you had a million pounds, what would you do with it?
8. Who do you know that is good with money, and why?
9. Would you rather spend everything you have before you die, or leave something behind for your loved ones?
10. What is the most you have ever spent on one item, and why?
11. Would you spend your last money on your guilty pleasure?
12. Where do you want to be financially in the next five years?

13. What is your financial priority right now?
14. What's the best quote about money you have ever heard?
15. Who is the most influential person you know?

Now try some of your own questions.

1. _____

2. _____

3. _____

4. _____

5. _____

CHAPTER 8

FAMILY AND FINANCE

> *'One of the greatest gifts you can give your children is a financial head start.'*

STARTING AND SUPPORTING A FAMILY FINANCIALLY

Your family is priceless, but there's no denying raising a family could leave you pinching the pennies. According to a 2019 report by the Child Poverty Action Group (CPAG), the average cost of raising a child to 18 was a staggering £185,413 for lone parent families and £152,747 for couples. One could argue that the cost of raising a child is more expensive than buying a house. These figures may sound daunting and if you haven't yet started a family, that might well be enough to scare you off, but rest assured this section will help you plan with confidence. If you have children, you may have already felt the pinch on your finances, especially if you had not planned and allocated money to cover the additional costs. Even the most prepared parent can still find things tricky, particularly when unexpected expenses jump up and take you by surprise, such as childcare costs, clothes and shoes that are outgrown so quickly and the extra room you have to book on holiday to accommodate your growing family. It all adds up!

With so many outgoings to consider, it is important to know where to draw the line. This chapter will help you understand the right financial planning to adopt for your family, and some of the costs you may encounter and how you can factor them into your budget, essentially laying a sound foundation for your family's future. Here are 10 top tips to help rein in the family finances.

1. Prepare and plan for a baby

Preparing for a newborn is full of checklists and plans, and a financial plan is just as crucial as cribs and childcare. Whether it's your first or third child, this should be a time of excitement and joy with lots to think about, from prams and car seats to bottles, nappies and toys. It's natural for parents to have financial concerns that can send you into panic mode, which does no one any good. What you need is a baby budget to paint a clear picture of your family finances. As well as factoring in all the additional expenses, you may need to adjust your budget to account for reduced income due to new work patterns or leaving work for some time.

A baby budget will allow you to remain calm, giving you more quality time with your newborn. The Money Advice Service website has a useful baby cost calculator, to help you work out the initial costs for a new baby and budget effectively. It is worth working out your expenses (one-off, ongoing and discretionary – see below) at least a year in advance, including other costs you may encounter such as a blessing, your first family holiday and even their first birthday party. It may seem far ahead, but time goes swiftly, and babies grow fast, so make this one less thing off the list of worries. Having children is about prioritising, which could mean a whole lot of sacrificing and a new way of life. However, you want to strike a balance as it's important to still try to do the things you love and enjoy while maintaining the day-to-day needs and contributing toward your baby's future. Separate your baby budget into three separate categories:

1. One-off expenses (medical bills, pram, cot, baby room decor, car seat)
2. Ongoing essentials (nappies, clothing, food, childcare)

3. Discretionary expenses (baby parties, holidays, cute pairs of designer shoes they will outgrow in a month)

Once you've set a baby budget, be prepared to make changes along the way, as things can be unpredictable. Your baby may grow out of their cot sooner than you think or potty training might take longer than you expected. So be flexible!

2. Consider childcare costs

If you return to work after having children almost half of your spending as a parent will go towards childcare. According to research by the Trades Union Congress (TUC), since 2008 the cost of childcare has risen four times faster than wages. Money Helper states that the current average childcare cost for a child under two is £138 per week part-time (25 hours) and £263 per week full-time (50 hours). So, if you have two children in full-time care, that would work out as £526 per week, which seems outrageous compared to the average UK weekly salary of £534 (ONS). Fortunately, you now have the option to make use of tax-free childcare and universal credit if eligible. It's also worth building a community of friends or family that can help out when needed to reduce the childcare cost burden.

3. Expense for education

School may be the greatest days of your child's life, but as a parent you still have so much to think about in terms of costs. New uniform, school shoes, stationery, books and school trips can all add up quickly. There are ways to reduce these expenses, such as buying uniforms from supermarkets or second-hand sales at the school, or making packed lunches instead of spending in the school canteen.

4. Keep an eye on household spending

According to the Office for National Statistics (ONS), the average household spent an estimated £558 per week in 2021. That figure includes food, clothing, bills, transportation and fuel, goods and services, recreational care and miscellaneous (personal care). It's always worth tracking your expenses month by month, looking for deals to stock up on essentials when they're on offer and shopping around for the best price on your energy bills to keep costs lower. Get the children involved by getting them into the practice of searching for offers on the weekly family shop, understanding the importance of turning the lights off to save electricity and being mindful of their water usage. If possible, opt to walk to school; children love it, and it's a great way to keep healthy while cutting down your monthly fuel bill.

5. Identify interests and hobbies
Depending on your child's interests, clubs and activities can be costly. When children are young, it's not unusual as a parent to sign them up for everything from swimming lessons, gymnastics and other sports to drama clubs and music tuition; after all, we want the best for them. However, this can take a toll on your finances and so it might be worth understanding what your child is really interested in and what they enjoy most and stick to those only. It's also worth checking out what after-school clubs your child's school runs as some will be free or at a discount.

6. Consider the cost of clothes
Raising a child from 0–18 is an expensive business – and creates big piles of washing! But washing is not the only thing that will leave you spinning. According to a study conducted by Money Supermarket in 2020, the average cost of children's clothes aged 2–13 was £11,723 for girls and £5,887 for boys (excluding footwear). Before you think of throwing the towel in, there are ways you can keep this cost down. Accepting hand-me-downs and buying second-hand clothes, especially when your kids are young, will save you hundreds of pounds. If you prefer buying off the

shelf, ensure that you shop around for the best prices and try shopping out of season – you are likely to bag some bargains. For example, buy winter coats in summer and shorts in winter.

7. Budget for birthdays and celebrations
Planning parties and buying presents for the big day takes a lot of preparation and money. Budgeting in advance can help, and if you're able to shop around for gifts at the best price, hire venues for parties and book trips as far in advance as possible, it's likely to come at a discount. Save money on expensive birthday cakes by having a go at making your own – children generally don't care about perfectly iced creations and homemade is so much cheaper.

8. Look for offers on leisure and days out
During half term and holidays, children will want to be entertained. A day out to the zoo, soft play centre, or simply a trip to the cinema can be costly. Put together a fun activities calendar with your little one(s) and use this as a way to plan your budget too. Don't forget, vouchers, offers and discounted tickets can help you save a little extra cash, so look out for offers online.

9. Monitor pocket money
Pocket money can be a great way to teach your children how to handle money from an early age – and take responsibility for household tasks such as cleaning their bedrooms and laundry duties. However, pocket money can add up, regardless of how much you give. Ensure you include the amount you give in your monthly budgets and try to stick to a set amount each month, so it's easy to track. Also, encourage children to save a proportion of their pocket money for things they really want.

10. Bundle tech gadgets
They say the older your child gets, the more they cost. Once you get to the in-between and teenage years, the cost of tech will go

up in your household: a game console or even a phone costs
hundreds of pounds. According to Money Supermarket, the total
cost parents spend on technology for children to the age of 16 is
£6,862 for girls and £7,795 for boys. Putting all your family's tech
gadgets on a plan can help with costs like TV deals and phone
contracts, while using apps that sell good condition second-hand
tech could save you loads.

FOUR STEPS TO TEACHING
YOUR CHILD MONEY VALUES

Believe it or not, investing and nurturing your child's values
around money can offer a huge return in the long run. Teaching
the value of money to your children isn't an overnight process
as different methods will apply, depending on age. The process
will take effect over several years, starting from preschool through
to teens and early adulthood. So, don't give up too early or don't
worry even if your children are older. If you haven't started, it's
never too late. Start with the basics!

1. Don't buy everything they ask for
This is not only for the benefit of your bank balance but will help
your children value what is important. Before splashing out on
the latest toy or game for Christmas, show them what else the
money can buy. This is an essential way of helping children
understand money and value. Your child may have their heart set
on a toy that costs £100; make them explore several cheaper items
they may also like. Alternatively, an iPhone costing the best part
of £800 may be at the top of their list but you could gently point
out that this is equivalent to 32 driving lessons (based on the
average cost of £25 per lesson) or even a deposit on a car. The
bottom line is, if you want your children to understand the value
of money, you must instil it from a young age.

2. Stick to your guns

You must remain consistent and practise what you preach. Don't be afraid to show children that money doesn't grow on trees; it takes hard work to achieve things we want in life. Too often Santa Claus or the Tooth Fairy take a whole lot of the credit, making it difficult for them to understand that, in fact, it's you who is the real hero. Try being more open about the things you do, the money you spend, and the sacrifices you make to ensure they have and enjoy the things they love and hopefully appreciate.

3. Set a budget

Set a budget for the items on their never-ending wish list and let them work towards it, either by doing chores or saving up their pocket money. There is something about appreciating an item more when you've contributed towards its purchase. Encourage them to compare costs online, so they don't overspend. You want them to find the best deals on what they want and avoid impulse purchases that will be tossed aside in a matter of days. Get them to note down three good reasons why they want something before it's purchased.

4. Reward

If children are good with money, you should reward them as you would do with schoolwork. By doing so, it's clear in their minds that they have done something well. It then becomes something they enjoy rather than a chore. You can create a reward chart for their saving or good money habits. By teaching your children good money habits when they're young, it will likely remain with them for the rest of their lives – and that really is worthwhile. If you have already started to teach your children the importance of budgeting and money, you should reward yourself. You have already laid the foundation to moulding a more financially responsible adult.

INVESTING IN YOU AND
YOUR FAMILY'S FUTURE

According to the London School of Economics, people in their twenties and early thirties are believed to be the first generation in meaningful history to be less affluent than their parents' generation. It is a crucial reason why planning your family wealth is more important now than ever before. It doesn't mean your children will not be highly successful, but you want to give them the best foundation to avoid financial hardship. Since 2008, we have experienced major financial changes, from interest rate cuts to buoyed financial markets, fuelled property prices and the rise of technology. It's no surprise that young adults don't see the benefits in saving, find it hard to invest, struggle to get on the property ladder or find a sustainable job. This section will help you explore ways that you can provide support to reduce the wealth gap in your family and offer greater prospects for your child or children.

Average cost of raising a child to 21

According to Liverpool Victoria (insurance company), in 2016 the average cost of raising a child to 21 broke down as follows:

CATEGORY	AMOUNT (2016)
Childcare and babysitting	£70,466
Education*	£74,430
Food	£19,004
Clothing	£10,942
Holidays	£16,882
Hobbies and toys	£9,307
Leisure and recreation	£7,464
Pocket money	£4,614
Furniture	£3,408
Personal	£1,130
Other (includes driving lessons, first car, birthday and Christmas presents)	£14,195
Total	£231,842

* Does not include private school fees but does include day-to-day costs associated with going to school (school trips, textbooks, uniform, school lunches) and university tuition fees. Sending a child to private school would add, on average, £141,863 for a child attending day school, or £260,927 for a child boarding at school, to the overall cost of raising a child, according to the Centre for Economics and Business Research.

* The figures provided are based on a study of a group of people and may vary depending on individual circumstances.

There's no denying the eye-watering sum of raising a child, especially if you have more than one. However, if you divide the total of £231,842 over 21 years, it equates to £11,040 a year, which is easier to digest.

ADDITIONAL COSTS YOU MAY NEED TO FACTOR IN

Of course, if you have done a good job raising your child to adult years, you may feel that your work is done – and rightfully so. But with many more young adults still dependent on their parents, it's worthwhile exploring some of the other costs that might come into play.

DRIVING LESSONS
£1,250
Auto Express 2019

UNIVERSITY TUITION FEES
£27,750
The World University Rankings

FIRST CAR
£5,000
The World University Rankings

FAMILY HOLIDAYS
£5,000
Jess Finch

WEDDING
£31,975
Hitched Pye, 2019

FIRST HOME
£27,750
Finder Boyle, 2020

Of course, you may not foot the bill for all of these costs, but it's surely worth considering what your goals are for your children, to set the foundation for their future. Have meaningful discussions to steer them in the right direction and find out what their priorities are. After all, one of the biggest influences on a child's money habits will be the attitude of their parents.

Investing in your child's future – the three paths

It has become clear there is a battle between **baby boomers** (fifties to mid-sixties) and **millennials** (early twenties to early forties) over wealth. The Bank of Mum and Dad is a fine example of the peace treaty that exists – but as a parent how do you avoid falling into this trap? Investing in your children starts from opening their first bank account (ideally, as young as possible). Every parent wants their children to have the best possible start in life, and there is no better way than a sound financial plan – and the foundation is saving. You may be considering the following:

1. Education fund

Covers tuition fees, school activities, trips and donations, which mount up over time. Therefore, it makes sense to set up a savings pot to cover these ongoing expenses. The ideal account for this is a general child saving account, due to the easy access.

2. Future fund

Covers all the other sizeable costs such as university fees, a wedding or helping with a deposit on their first home. The ideal way of saving for these events is in long-term accounts such as a Junior ISA (see page 88), or your own ISA if you wish to have more control. Some accounts may have access restrictions, normally until the child is 18, so only put in what you don't need in the short term.

3. Children's pension

Did you know you can invest in a pension from the day your child is born? You can invest up to £3,600 per year (this figure is based on the tax year 22/23 and can change in future) and receive tax relief so you only physically pay £2,880 net. Investing in a pension for your child may be a long stretch but is a great way to pave the road for their future.

Suppose you contribute £3,600 per year consecutively for 18 years into a child's pension; you could accumulate a pension pot of £425,000 for your child. Here's the breakdown:

- You invest £300 a month (gross payment including the government tax relief), meaning you contribute the maximum £3,600 each tax year, from birth until your child reaches the age of 18, at which point you stop contributing.
- After 18 years, £64,800 will have been invested, but the returns (less the charges) will have boosted the fund to £91,800. (This assumes an average investment return of 4.5% a year and an investment-management charge of 0.75% a year.)
- If this £91,800 is then held in the pension from 18–60 (42 years), with the same investment return and charges, it will be worth about £425,000 by the age of 60.

(Source: Aviva)

In that case, your child could benefit from a pension pot of £425,000. How fantastic would that be to give your child that kind of financial freedom, or just imagine if your parents had done this for you? Note that the money can't be accessed until they reach pension age, so be confident that you can commit for the long road. Remember, pensions are subject to risk and growth is not guaranteed. (The figures provided are an example for financial guidance only. You should always seek professional advice.)

Don't lose track of yourself!
The best gift you can give a child or children is for you to be financially secure in your own right. Then you can allow them to focus on their future, without them worrying about their parents. You might well put your children's priorities before your own, which is quite natural, but never forget how important it is for you to continue to **stay on track.**

A SIMPLE ROUTINE GUIDE TO MANAGING YOUR MONEY EFFECTIVELY

Set a daily financial affirmation as soon as you wake up

Listen to a financial podcast while you get ready

Read, blog or listen to the news on your commute to work

Open a conversation about money while you eat lunch

Read or listen to a finance audiobook on the commute home

Have a cup of tea while doing your home admin

Update your finance tracker while listening to your favourite song

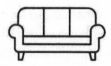

Relax and unwind – read this book or another fave!

At bedtime give your financial affirmation a big tick and set a to-do list for the next day

CHAPTER 9

SAFEGUARDING YOUR FUTURE

> *'Don't leave anything to chance –
> protect the ones you love with insurance.'*
> —EVE WILSON

PROTECTING WHAT'S IMPORTANT – WHAT IS THE BACKUP PLAN IF YOU ARE SICK, UNABLE TO WORK OR DIE?

You cannot predict the future, but you can certainly prepare for it. You may be accustomed to the likes of home and car insurance but safeguarding your most valuable possession – you and your family – should not be overlooked. Protection acts as a pillar that upholds your financial planning and prevents all your plans from collapsing in the worst cases, just like a plan B!

Life insurance is essential *not* preferential

As sad as it may seem, there is one thing that life promises, and that's death. Therefore, life cover is essential to everyone, especially if you have financial dependants such as children or a spouse who will suffer financially if you die. Likewise, if you have large debts that you prefer not to leave behind. As difficult as it always is to discuss these options, life cover will provide peace of mind – and once it's done it's done! It can be used to pay off your mortgage, help you and your family maintain their standard of living or simply cover funeral costs in the event of a death.

Life insurance is likely to have free built-in benefits, such as terminal illness (when a doctor's report states that life expectancy is less than 12 months) or accidental death cover (death caused by accident). These benefits should not be confused with critical illness or income protection, which is described below. There are also additional benefits you can include, such as waiver of premium (covers the monthly premiums after a set period if you are unable to work due to accident or sickness). Life cover is affordable especially if taken while young and in good health and can start from as little as £6 per month. However, the cost will depend on age, health, smoker status and other factors such as body mass index figures. So, everyone's insurance will be different. However, as a rule of thumb, the earlier you take out cover, the cheaper the cost. Here are some life covers that may suit your needs:

- **Level Term Assurance** The benefit amount remains the same throughout the term, usually suited for family protection or interest-only mortgages. The cover provided is a lump sum, and you can select the amount of cover you want and when you want the cover to end. Most plans will typically coincide with the date your youngest child becomes financially independent or your mortgage ends. You can also opt for increasing term assurance for cover to increase in line with inflation.
- **Decreasing Assurance** The chosen cover reduces throughout the term, usually suited to cover repayment mortgages or a decreasing estate (for inheritance tax purposes). The amount of cover will decrease in line with your mortgage and therefore will naturally end at the end of a mortgage term or when the mortgage is paid up.
- **Family Income Benefit (FIB)** FIB can be life cover, critical illness cover or both, and pays a regular amount as opposed to a lump sum, normally reflecting the annual income of the insured. It is designed to maintain the family's standard of living in an unforeseen event and is excellent if you prefer not to leave a lump sum, or you or your financial dependants are not great with money. However, you do have the option to compute to a lump sum if needed.

- **Whole of Life** A life cover with no expiration date, meaning it will pay out at the point of death, usually suited to cover funeral expenses or inheritance tax costs. These types of plans can include an investment value. This means that the premiums you have paid are placed in an investment fund. If the fund does well, the value of the lump sum your loved ones will receive increases. But if the fund does poorly, your premiums are likely to rise to make up the difference. You could also cash out on your investments yourself. For these reasons, they are more expensive than assurance type plans.

Critical illness cover (CIC)

Critical illness cover pays out a lump sum if you suffer a specified critical or serious illness such as heart attack, stroke or cancer, usually within 14 days of diagnosis. Most insurances cover 40–80 specified illnesses. Some insurers offer more comprehensive cover than others, so be sure to do your research. Most CIC plans will include a number of minor illnesses they will pay out for, although the amounts are likely to be a set percentage of the cover. CIC plans are likely to include free built-in benefits such as accident hospitalisation benefit (a small sum paid if you are in hospital with physical injuries for a minimum of several days, immediately following an accident) and children's critical illness cover (a set amount, usually £25,000 or 25% of the benefit, paid out if a child under 18 is diagnosed with a critical illness). You can also include additional benefits for a nominal cost, such as total and permanent disability – a benefit that pays out an agreed sum of money in the event of an illness or injury that results in permanent incapacity – and fracture cover (provides cover if you are unable to work due to bone fractures)

The amount of cover you need will depend on your debts, financial dependants, work benefits, other insurances, and your budget. You can decide on whatever end date you choose, although most plans will coincide with your retirement date. It is more expensive than life insurance as the risks it imposes are higher. However, unlike life insurance, you can benefit while you're still around, and it can be used in such cases to pay off your mortgage so you can focus on your health or cover medical expenses. It is important to note that it will not pay out for all illnesses and will only cover those specified. You also may have exclusions that apply if you have a pre-existing condition.

True story:

Jacqueline, a single mother with four children (aged 16, 9, 5 and 1), was diagnosed with cancer at the age of 35. Sadly, she died suddenly at age 36 with no cover in place. This tragic event had life-changing effects on her family and children. The following shows the possible outcomes if she were adequately protected.

- **Life cover/Family income benefit** This would have paid a lump sum or regular income to maintain a standard of living and cover education costs for the children following her death.
- **Critical illness cover** This would have likely paid out within days of the diagnosis, which would have allowed Jacqueline to cover her and her family's ongoing expenses, including childcare for the children and medical bills including best care and treatment (providing the amount of cover was sufficient).
- **Private medical care**: This would have provided Jacqueline with fast access to private health care and covered any high or unexpected medical bills, which can make all the difference.

* For confidentiality, some of the details have been changed.
*All claims are subject to eligibility. Your provider may fail to pay out on death or illness if you have not been truthful regarding your health (at application) or if the cause of a death or illness is excluded from the plan. For example, some plans will not pay out for suicide. You should check the terms and conditions of your insurance to understand inclusions and exclusions.

Income protection

This provides a supplementary income should you be unable to work due to an accident or sickness. You can generally get cover up to 60–70% of your income to help you cope with day-to-day costs while employment income has ceased. You can set a term of your choice, but the cover will typically coincide with your retirement or mortgage end date. You have the flexibility to select a start date or deferral period (period you wait before receiving income), which can start from day one, which is ideal if you have no savings or other means of income. Alternatively, you may wish to choose an extended deferral period, such as three, six or twelve months if you have adequate savings or cover at work. For example, if you have six months of full pay from your employer, you won't need cover to start until the income stops; therefore, a six-month deferral period would suffice. The longer the deferral period, the cheaper your monthly premium.

Income protection can also be considered to specifically cover mortgage payments only, known as Mortgage Payment Protection Insurance or MPPI, which may also cover you for unemployment cover (involuntary redundancy only). However, due to the controversy around MPPI, these products are scarce and can generally only be taken at the point of a new mortgage.

Private medical insurance

If you live in the UK, you benefit from free healthcare from the NHS. However, private medical insurance could be right up your street if you prefer a more VIP service with shorter waiting times. It provides access to medical specialists in private hospitals with a speedy service. There are also several add-ons you can consider, such as dental and optical care, as well as a worldwide cover. You can even cover the whole family, in which case you're likely to get a delightful discount.

* The following insurance figures, including benefits, terms, specified illnesses, cover amounts, deferral periods and terms and conditions, are

subject to future changes, and the amount of cover and benefits you receive will vary depending on choice or advice, and the cost (including benefits) will differ depending on the provider.

* The insurance information provided is for general guidance, and you should seek financial advice for personal recommendations.

Beware of identical insurances

It is possible you have some insurance and don't even know; this is because they may be hidden in a savings plan or a bank account, which makes it easy for you to duplicate cover. The list below shows some instances where this may crop up. When considering insurance, you may want to factor in these other insurances; however, if you want long-term peace of mind, it may be worth keeping your paid insurances separate.

CRITERIA	BENEFITS
Life cover	**Death in service** Most employers will typically offer a multiple of your salary ranging between two and five times your salary, paid as a lump sum in the event of your death. So, if you earn £30,000, you may be covered for £60,000–£150,000. DIS is a benefit in kind and therefore will no longer be available if you leave the company, or the company decides to withdraw the benefit. To find out the value of your DIS, check your employment contract or contact your HR department.
	Pension Some pensions will have a life cover built in, which is common with employer-based pensions. It's worth double-checking!
	Investment bond If you have an investment bond or endowment you will likely have life cover built in and in the event of death it will usually pay out a similar amount to the money invested. For example, if you have £100,000 invested, you could expect to receive £100,000 upon death (terms may vary depending on the plan and provider).

CRITERIA	BENEFITS
Income protection	**Employer sick pay** A benefit offered by employers to their employees to provide an income for a set period if off work due to sickness. The period of pay typically ranges between one and six months full pay, with some employers offering longer terms with less pay, i.e. 50% of your salary. However, this is becoming scarce, with many employers opting for short-term cover or statutory sick pay only.
	Statutory sick pay (SSP) The government will pay you money if you are sick and unable to work. So why do you need additional cover? Well, this is because SSP is unfathomable and is likely not adequate to maintain your standard of living. It is worth noting that some income protection covers will affect your state benefit entitlement in the event of a claim.
Private medical insurance	**Employer private medical insurance** A common benefit that your employer may offer. However, it is likely to be at a cost, although it will usually be cheaper than a personal PMI, so it's one worth taking.
Other insurances	**Current account** Your current account may offer insurance such as travel insurance, accidental cover and mobile phone cover free of charge. However, some current accounts will charge a monthly fee to run, so technically you are paying for the added benefits.

Now you understand your safeguarding options it's time to think about your own personal protections. Are they suitable in terms of will they pay out when you need it most? Do they need reviewing? The chances are if you have had some protection in place for five years or more the likelihood is things may have changed in your personal circumstances. Whether it's a change in income, expenditure or a new baby your protections will need updating to accurately reflect your needs.

> *'Protection is the first necessity*
> *of opulence and luxury.'*
> —JOSEPH CONRAD

CHAPTER SUMMARY

List three things you are proud you have accomplished after reading this chapter.

1.

2.

3.

Now list three things you will look forward to doing differently after reading this chapter.

1.

2.

3.

What one thing in this chapter inspired you to change the way you think and feel?

Safeguarding Your Future: signs and signals

Here are five signals to stay **on track** and five signs to prevent you falling **off track**.

ON TRACK if you	OFF TRACK if you
Adequately protect you and your family against an unforeseen event	Fail to review your insurances – at least every three years
Place your life insurance in trust	Remain with the same insurer for years with no loyalty benefit
Prioritise your insurance as an essential expense	Think protection is too expensive
Factor in the cover you receive from work or make use of tax-deductible expenses if self-employed	Believe you will live for ever and never get sick
Shop around for the best insurance	Fail to invest in your child/children's future

You have arrived at the final stop on the Safeguarding Your Future journey. Remember to take all the knowledge you have gained with you on your next journey

MY TOP 10 MONEY MUST-HAVES

You can achieve these at any time, and in no particular order, so no pressure!

1. **Emergency fund** – at least three months of income saved.

2. **Enjoyable expenses account** – separate from your main account.

3. **Finance tracker** – use the Budget Buddy on page 281.

4. **Goal savings account** – to fund all your dream goals.

5. **A shredder** – to keep your financial paperwork tidy and up to date.

6. **Financial folders** – to keep all financial paperwork or (online) files organised.

7. **Financial notebook** – to list all personal financial information.

8. **Financial feed** – to provide you with regular financial news and important information.

9. **Financial accountability partner** – this could be a notebook, friend or a financial adviser.

10. **Direct debits** – to ensure bills are paid on time, and to help you improve your money management and boost your credit.

Honestly, it took me years to achieve everything, but I did it, and you can too! You have the list, and there's no greater feeling than working towards achieving even one step. Challenge yourself and see how many you can achieve in a year!

Can you think of some other financial essentials?

1. _____

2. _____

3. _____

4. _____

5. _____

CHAPTER 10

DERAILING FINANCIAL DILEMMAS

> 'Instead of focusing on circumstances that you cannot change, focus strongly and powerfully on the circumstances that you can.'
> —JOY PAGE

What do you do when life throws you unexpected curveballs, as it so often does, and how do you protect your finances? Conversely, how do you maintain wealth when, or if you receive it unexpectedly, especially at a young age? This chapter will help you keep control of your money if you are hit by one of the dreaded DDBP – Divorce, Debt, Bereavement and a Pandemic. It will also explore how to remain financially focused during victorious ventures.

DEBT AND HOW TO DEAL WITH IT

Break the chain

People get into debt for different reasons, but a sudden change in circumstance is a common trap fallen into by many. If you have incurred debt, your top priority should be how to get out of it. It can be the hardest thing to avoid, and falling into debt can happen to anyone, at any point in life. The key is to change your money habits as soon as possible. We live in an economy where having debt is the norm, but let's be clear: debt is a finance issue that needs controlling. No one feels good about debt, regardless of how much debt they are in, and so you'll be pleased to know the problem is solvable, whatever the scale. This section guides you through overcoming that overwhelming overdraft to ultimately reducing and eradicating the weight of debt you may be carrying.

Find the root of the problem

One of the main reasons people find it difficult to get out of debt is because they don't know how they got there in the first place. Identifying exactly how you accumulated your debt will give you a clear idea of how to move forward. There are various reasons why you might be finding it hard to break the debt chain, which include:

TEMPTATION

- Problem: You are an impulse buyer, and you find it difficult to say no.
- Solution: Try to set boundaries to avoid giving in to temptations.

ADDICTION

- Problem: You may have a debt addiction and find yourself accumulating debt for no reason
- Solution: Speak with a counsellor or therapist to help you control any underlying issues – it's likely to stem from somewhere.

POOR MONEY MANAGEMENT

- Problem: There is no limit to your spending, which is causing your debt to rack up.
- Solution: Go over the chapter on Budgeting (see page 43) in detail to improve this area.

SOCIAL INFLUENCES

- Problem: You succumb to peer pressure, which can be strong and hard to avoid. It may be friends or family who also have huge debts, so it becomes normalised and 'not too bad'.

- Solution: Change your social circle or make drastic changes yourself and potentially be a role model to them.

> *When you don't have debt, your money can do anything you want it to.*

My top 10 ways to depart from debt
Once you get to the root of your problem, you're halfway to sorting it. A watchful eye will also prevent additional debt while you're still tackling it. Debt prevents you from achieving your financial goals, so follow the next steps to break the chain.

1. Own up to it
The first step to freeing yourself from debt is owning up to it. One thing you don't want to do is shy away. Many people are afraid of addressing liabilities and often hide away from red letters. If this is you, then it's time to come out of the closet. The worst thing you can do is avoid your debts, thinking they'll just go away. You must tackle them head-on to be debt-free. Start by listing all your debts one by one from loans, credit cards – even the money you owe family. Taking responsibility will not only help you get rid of debt but will make you feel much better. Use the debt thermometer on page 287 to list your debts and keep track of your progress to becoming debt-free.

2. Set a debt deadline
Set a deadline for when you want to be debt-free. How long will it take you to get there? How will you feel once you have arrived? Work out how long it will take to pay off all debts, and how you can realistically afford to do that. Once you identify the timescale, you can start to plan, and eventually create division between you and your debts.

3. Spend less

Debt is often a result of spending more money than you can afford to. So, one of the easiest ways to reduce it is to cut down on spending. Use your Budget Buddy (see page 281) to help you avoid these issues and build suitable savings to provide a financial cushion in times of need. If you are serious about clearing debts, you should aim to reduce all unnecessary expenses and keep the end goal in mind – being debt-free!

4. Avoid further borrowing

Never borrow more debt to clear existing debts; you will end up going round and round in a vicious circle with little progress, which is just torture! It's so much easier to reduce and clear debt if you stop adding to it. There's no point in clearing a lump sum off your credit card only to keep using it again. If you want to break the cycle, it's time to get organised, focused and think ahead. Do yourself a favour and cut up your credit cards or don't leave home with them!

Let's take an example: you may be planning a holiday and think it's a great idea to put the contents of your suitcase on a credit card. However, a credit card purchase of £500 could end up costing you £1,000 and can take 100 months to clear (based on a minimum of £10 monthly payments). Instead, you could save £100 per month for five months and achieve the same goal without the added costs. By saving for something as opposed to putting it on the credit card, you are more likely to buy things you want, rather than be seduced by impulse purchases that may have little value in years to come. Besides, if you go to work just to spend all your income on bills and debt, you make your journey to financial freedom strenuous.

5. Settle small debts

Put your debts in order of priority and see the magic happen before your eyes. The bigger your debt, i.e. a mortgage, the lower the interest rate, so if you have small debt outstanding, get that paid off first as it probably has a high interest rate. Small debts are the easiest to remove, and doing so will give you a sense of satisfaction. It will also release some disposable income that you can add towards other debts to get them cleared more quickly. Any debts with interest above 10% can be excessive when you are struggling to clear things up.

6. Fix a monthly payment

Aim to fix a set amount each month; this will make it less compli-cated for you to manage. It may mean transferring your credit card debt to a personal loan or paying a set amount above the monthly minimum payment. A set amount will help you keep track of your budget and give you a clear idea of when the debt will be removed.

7. Consolidate

If you can consolidate all debts into one place, you're going to save interest and make life easier. Having too many debts with different providers can be confusing and overwhelming. Consider an option that freezes the interest on your liabilities, such as a 0% interest rate credit card to give you enough time to clear debts without paying interest. Alternatively, if you have debts with double-figure interest rates, try consolidating them all into a personal loan to reduce the interest.

8. Downgrade

If you have a house that's bigger than you need or a car that's too flashy for your income, it might be time to downgrade. Getting your life on track should be your priority, not appearances. Downsizing doesn't mean you are going backwards – it means you can take control of your future!

9. Switch lenders

When in debt, don't let lender loyalty get in the way. Make sure you have a good look at the market to see if you're getting the best deal. Many comparison sites make this task easy. Simply enter the details of your existing credit card or loan and see what the market has to offer. If you can pay less interest on your outstanding debt, it will help you pay off your debts a lot quicker. Moving may seem a tedious task, but most providers will do all the work for you.

10. Stick to the plan

If you see further debt coming your way, turn the steering wheel and head in the other direction. Adding to debts can be impulsive and addictive for some. Stay mindful of your spending and protect yourself in the right financial way, so you drive down the deficit.

 FOR A PERSONAL VIEW: Complete the debt thermometer tracker (see page 287)

> *Don't give up what you want in FUTURE for what you want NOW.*

Till debt do us part

Believe it or not, debt is not tied to you legally like a marriage and if you feel your debt is spiralling beyond control, speak to your debtors early. Companies are generally more concerned with your willingness to pay, so you may be able to come to an affordable agreement, which will immediately take the pressure off and allow you to feel back in control.

Should I still save while in debt?

The answer is yes! Don't forget about savings while paying off debts; you want to achieve a balance. However, it depends on the amount of debt and the interest rate being charged. If interest rates are low, you may be better off clearing debts first. It might seem sufficient to put all your disposable money towards debts. Still, you may prioritise financial goals overpaying debts, as if you have no savings, you could find yourself unexpectedly back to square one. Ideally, it's good to do both to maintain financial stability and not lose sight of financial goals. Put a priority on clearing debts with high interest first, then continue saving. There's no point being debt-free in future only to find you have no reserves to help you achieve your future goals or to cover you in an emergency. If this is not possible, you should clear debts first so you can fully focus on your financial goals without being weighed down by debt.

The last resort

Suppose you are buried in debt, and after exploring all the above options find you are still struggling financially. In that case, you may want to consider one of the following options. The worst thing you can do is suffer in silence as there are alternative options, even in the worst-case scenarios (see below). However, these are last resort options and should only be considered after expert advice and with your full understanding.

DEBT MANAGEMENT PLAN

An agreement between you and the creditor to pay off all your debts, by paying a reduced monthly amount – helpful if you are suffering short-term financial issues. Be aware: some creditors may charge a fee.

INDIVIDUAL VOLUNTARY AGREEMENT (IVA)

This is a formal legally binding debt solution that allows you to pay back your debts over a period, usually five to six years. If approved, IVAs will free the interest and charges on your debt. Your IVA will be held on your credit file for six years and will also be held on the public register, which may restrict you from getting further credit.

BANKRUPTCY

This option allows you to wipe away all your debts and restart with a clean slate. However, your credit rating and financial standing will be severely affected for many years after filing, and this will prevent you from getting a mortgage or starting a business. Bankruptcy should only be considered if you are in severe financial difficulty and cannot see that any improvement to your circumstances is likely. If you are worried about debt or struggling see page 297.

DIVORCE AND SEPARATION

Going through a divorce is likely to be the biggest legal, financial and emotional stress you will go through, and the decision can adversely affect your finances. Whether you were together for one year or ten, it is never easy, regardless of how and why the relationship broke down. It's not just you and your partner going separate ways but your finances and possibly your family too. So how do you come out on the other side without completely uprooting? You may be coming to terms with co-parenting, being a single parent or being single, which can unsettle you and your finances. You want to ensure you avoid acting with emotion when making financial decisions and you may need emotional support to deal with the stress, so don't be afraid to reach out to friends, relatives or a therapist to deal with your emotions first. Protecting you and your finances is critical; you want to be treated fairly and avoid being left financially disadvantaged. Try to remain positive even if things seem like they are up in the air, without beating yourself up. Once ready, you should start by making a financial checklist of the things that need addressing.

Contact your bank and creditors

If you have joint accounts with your ex-partner, the first thing you want to do is contact all lenders and inform them of your situation – particularly important if the divorce isn't amicable (although this may be easier said than done!). You can request for the account to be changed to your sole name or freeze the account if you are worried your ex-partner will access funds without your consent. However, your ex-partner must agree and cooperate.

If you have joint debts such as credit cards you are equally responsible for the total borrowing, so it's wise to ask for the card back, so there is no further spending without you being aware, or at least agree who is responsible for paying the debts. Again, you need approval and agreement, and so if this is not possible, you should speak with the debt providers to put a block on the debts until the situation is resolved.

Protect your home (if owned)

More than likely, the property is likely to be the biggest financial debate in a divorce, especially if it's held in joint names, and therefore an agreement must be made as to how the property will be shared or who will remain in the property. Alternatively, it may be owned in one person's name or by a family member, normally a parent. You may decide to sell the property and share the profits 50/50. However, if there are children involved, you may both agree that one of you will remain in the home. Therefore, one will need to financially compensate the other with other financial resources such as cash, investments or releasing money from the property. In cases where a mutual agreement cannot be decided by both parties, the court will give the final verdict on how assets will be shared based on both parties' circumstances.

Protect your savings and investments

If you have savings in joint names, this may be easier to split fairly, although percentages can still vary. You may have been the most significant contributor to the joint savings and therefore require a more substantial share. Likewise, if you are left to look after children, you may also be entitled to a more significant proportion. However, if there are no complex circumstances, the simplest option is to split the joint savings down the middle.

Investments require a different strategy because the money is invested in stocks and shares, which are subject to market fluctuations (ups and downs). If you withdraw at the wrong time, you could end up with less than you invested. Take the following example:

> Conrad and Isabel jointly invested a lump sum of £50,000 into a General Investment Account in March 2018, accumulated from money given as wedding gifts. Unfortunately, the marriage went sour two years later, and they mutually agreed to split the money equally. They enquired about the value of their joint fund in March 2020 and discovered the current value had dropped to £42,500. They were told the reduction was due to a financial market downturn as a result of COVID-19, and that they had two options. They could either face the brunt and accept the loss (meaning their 50% share would have reduced from £25,000 to £21,250) or remain invested and wait for markets to return – with no specific time or guarantee.

Of course, if the divorce had occurred at a more favourable time, the circumstances would be more pleasant. If you are faced with circumstances like this, you should seek financial advice before making any rash decisions. If there is no urgent need for the money, you might consider waiting for markets to recover. Alternatively, you have the option to remain invested by merely transferring the account into your sole name if you want complete separation. If you decide to transfer your funds out this may incur capital gains tax, so be sure to double-check beforehand.

Refresh your budget
When going through changing circumstances that force your income or expenses to shift, it's a wise time to pay closer attention to your budget, to keep your finances on track. Regardless of

whether you are the breadwinner or a stay-at-home parent, you're likely to see a change in income after separating. It may be a result of additional childcare, reduced work hours or getting or paying financial support. Likewise, it may mean readjusting to a lifestyle you have to give up as a result of separating.

Major changes to your way of life can affect your behaviours and can lead to unconscious spending and overindulgence. It's easy to get lost in the moment when going through a stressful time, but thinking long-term and reviewing future goals will ground you and become the momentum you need to get things moving in the right direction.

Splitting your pensions – three options to consider

Splitting your pension is not as straightforward as splitting money in a bank account. The amounts that are provided are normally decided by the court and can be done in three ways as follows.

PENSION SHARING

Pension sharing is the common route as it is simple and straight-forward. The court will issue a **pension sharing order** (PSO), which will state the appropriate split for each party as a percentage or a specific amount. It provides a clean break for both parties on divorce, meaning each party can decide what to do with their share independently. However, it is not always possible to split pensions, and therefore the pension benefits remain with the former spouse's scheme, rather than being transferred to another plan (known as the Shadow Membership) – this is common with unfunded schemes such as NHS pensions.

Separating your finances may be more complicated if:

- You have a joint business
- One of you is financially dependent on the other
- One of you disagrees with the divorce
- The children are financially dependent on both parents
- The marriage has lasted five years or more

- One person has a medical problem or disability, which affects their ability to work
- One individual has more assets than the other. For example, one person may have a much larger pension pot

PENSION OFFSETTING

Allows other assets to be offset instead of the pension. In other words, one will keep their pension pot, and the other will keep the house. This option is popular as it provides a clean break for both parties. For example:

> Mark and Ellen have recently divorced. Mark is a doctor and has built up a healthy pension with a current pot worth £1,000,000. Ellen will keep the residential home worth £500,000 (50% of the pension), which is mortgage-free. She has little in her pensions but has plans to downsize in retirement and will use the profits to buy a rental property to provide income in retirement.

The court will ultimately consider all assets to ensure the split is fair. Due to this, it can be difficult to value some assets, especially if these are subject to fluctuation or under disguise. So, the pension may be the most valuable asset in the long run. If this option proves difficult, you may have the opportunity to use a pension sharing or earmarking option.

PENSION EARMARKING (ALSO KNOWN AS PENSION ATTACHMENT ORDER)

An earmarking order is where all or part of a pension is paid to the ex-spouse or civil partner when the pension is due to pay out. It may not be the most attractive option as it doesn't provide a clean break. There is an ongoing link between partners, and if the original owner of the pension decides to take benefits, the other spouse must take theirs simultaneously, which could cause tax disadvantages if the other person is still working. The member also decides on the investment strategy, so there may be little choice as to the risk or ethical preferences, and it is taxed on the original owner before funds are distributed.

Another consideration is that members of a final salary scheme could attempt to reduce benefits payable to their former spouse by opting out and starting a new pension plan. The court will ultimately decide the right amount that should go to each spouse. The following table shows when earmarking can and cannot be applied:

EARMARKING CAN BE APPLIED TO	EARMARKING DOES NOT APPLY TO
Pension income benefits	Basic State Pension
A tax-free cash lump sum	State Graduated Scheme
Death-in-service lump sum benefits	SERPS/S2P
A new pension (if transferred)	Death of the spouse

Note: Some of the terms and options may differ depending on where you live.

BEREAVEMENT – COPING WITH THE DEATH OF A LOVED ONE

The death of a loved one can significantly impact your finances, mental state and wellbeing. Sorting out your finances may be the last thing on your mind – this is all normal and very natural for someone grieving the loss of a loved one. However, losing track of your finances altogether will only add to your stress.

Managing all your finances may be an overwhelming task during a bereavement. If this is the case, don't be afraid to reach out to someone you trust for comfort and support. Once you feel ready to address your finances, focus on the more urgent issues first, such as paying your mortgage and staying up to date with household bills. Make it a priority to contact any providers you have financial dealings with, including the providers of the deceased (if they were your spouse). You want to inform them of your circumstances so they can offer support and protect your account (or the deceased) from any fraudulent activities. Most providers have policies in place for bereavements and vulnerable situations; they should work at your pace, so don't feel pressured or rushed. The next thing is to contact the local authority to see what financial support you may be entitled to, such as:

- **Bereavement Support Payment (BSP)** – Offered to the bereaved spouse of the deceased (subject to eligibility criteria).
- **Funeral Expense Payment** – Provides support if help is needed to pay for funeral arrangements.
- **Child's Funeral Fund** – Support for parents towards the funeral cost for a child who has died under the age of 18 or stillborn.
- **Guardian's Allowance** – Available to those bringing up a child whose parent or parents have died. It is a weekly tax-free amount, usually paid in addition to child benefit. However, you must meet the eligibility criteria to claim (the terms and eligibility criteria may differ depending on your jurisdiction).

Managing inheritance

You may have inherited some money from a loved one and find yourself in the position of having to decide when and how to deal with the money while possibly in an emotional and vulnerable state. It's a good idea to take a step back, breathe and think things through.

If you have inherited a lump sum through a trust, there may be legal rules to follow. For example, the trust may state what the money is to be used for, such as education or to buy a property, in which case the rules must strictly be adhered to unless you have a good reason not to. Otherwise, you are free to make your own decisions. The size of the sum will determine what you can do. You may be thinking of putting money aside for children's education, fulfilling a dream, or to simply ensure you have enough to live. If you have been left a substantial sum and are feeling too overwhelmed, speak with a legal or financial expert to help you make the right decisions.

There is no haste to get things started, but once you feel up to arranging your finances, put a plan in place. Your perspective on life may have changed, and this could influence previous goals you may have set. So, look at everything with a fresh pair of eyes and ensure your new financial plan works for you.

HANDLING YOUR MONEY DURING A PANDEMIC

If money worries are keeping you up at night, you are not alone. A pandemic can be an incredibly stressful time in a person's life, but it's not just health that suffers; it's your money too. COVID-19, in particular, brought on many unexpected changes in our lives, some we will never forget. It forced us to look into our finances differently, whether that was saving more, spending less or creating additional income streams. Everyone's financial situation is different, but here are a few case studies to show some of the examples I experienced with clients.

SUSAN: Lost her £100,000 job as an operations manager in an airline company. Susan wished she had put more in her emergency fund and was more serious about building savings. Unfortunately, she was left in a position where she could not maintain her living standards with no income coming in and insufficient savings. This brought on financial stress and anxiety as she had never experienced such an event. The lesson learned is: just because you have lots of money coming in, it doesn't mean it all has to go out. Financial security is key!

SARAH: Sarah was furloughed during the pandemic and continued to receive 80% of her salary; although her income was reduced, she was not financially disadvantaged. She saved by not spending money commuting, buying lunches at work and social nights out with friends. Sarah discovered she had an extra £300 disposable income. She decided to save this amount to boost her emergency fund and future savings. The lesson learned here is: maximise every financial opportunity you have; they may not come around often, so make the most of it!

SHOLA: As a self-employed virtual assistant Shola was able to continue working throughout the pandemic and saw an increase in her business as companies sought alternative options to fulfil their administration needs during COVID-19. She put her mortgage payments on hold for six months through a payment holiday. Even though she was receiving more money than usual, she wanted to keep all bills to a minimum and decided to reduce spending. This is because she is self-employed, and her income is not guaranteed. The lesson learned is: find ways to increase your income with a skill or passion; there is likely demand for your goods or service. Also, the key is to avoid increasing your expenses with your income.

TIPS FOR COPING FINANCIALLY DURING A PANDEMIC

Furloughed by your employer	• Check you have sick pay with your employer • Consider any schemes available to support staff • Maximise opportunities to build up an emergency fund or consider regular investing with any additional disposable income • Reduce unnecessary expenditure • Keep up with debt payments if you can
Self-employed	• Consider emergency credit to tide you over in shortfall months • Take advantage of schemes available for self-employed individuals • Reduce but maintain savings and investments if possible • Reduce unnecessary expenditure • Set an emergency plan of action for your business
Directors	• Seek grants and loans available • Consider emergency credit to tide you over in shortfall months • Reduce but maintain savings and investments if possible • Reduce unnecessary expenditure • Set an emergency plan of action for the business • Seek funding or grants for staff
Lost job	• Seek financial support from state benefit entitlements, friends or family • Contact creditors to put a pause on payments • Seek alternative methods to earn income • Retrain or study • Inform a mortgage provider, landlord or estate agent of your financial situation • Avoid depleting all emergency funds • Keep emotionally safe

Regardless of your current financial situation, it's important to know that you can turn things around and get back on top of your finances in no time. We have all experienced some changes as a result of a pandemic, so don't suffer in silence – try to open up to someone if you are struggling financially. Take this period as a major lesson; how would you manage things differently in future, and how can you manage your money better going forward to prepare you for such events? I know we don't want to prepare for another pandemic (and I sincerely hope we don't have to), but it's always better to be safe than sorry!

> *Let's normalise the fact that wealth is not about having lots of money, it's about having lots of options.*

CHAPTER SUMMARY

List three things you are proud you have accomplished after reading this chapter.

1. _____

2. _____

3. _____

Now list three things you will look forward to doing differently after reading this chapter.

1. _____

2. _____

3. _____

What one thing in this chapter inspired you to change the way you think and feel?

- -

Derailing Financial Dilemmas: signs and signals

Here are five signals to help you stay **on track** and five signs to prevent you falling **off track**.

ON TRACK if you	OFF TRACK if you
Take ownership of debts – create a debt plan	Shy away from your financial responsibilities
Communicate your financial needs through a divorce	Don't attempt to use the debt thermometer tool on page 287
Avoid emotions getting in the way of your financial decisions	Allow a divorce to leave you financially disadvantaged
Re-evaluate your finances during changing times	Don't reach out for help when needed
Take time out for yourself to recharge	Give up financially – there's always a way to turn things around

You have arrived at the final stop on your Derailing Financial Dilemmas journey. Remember to take all the knowledge you have gained with you on your next journey.

KEEP ON TRACK OF YOUR FINANCES

We naturally feel more confident and empowered when we know what's going on with our finances. So, it's important that you create a list of the various ways you can keep up to date and track your money. Choosing the right podcast or financial feed can give you the extra motivation you need to help you continue your financial freedom journey. I've listed my top seven.

MY TOP 7 WAYS TO KEEP ON TRACK OF MY FINANCES

1. Podcasts – Great for when you are on the move and you need a financial knowledge boost.
2. Blogs – There are some amazing financial bloggers out there to help you gain deeper insight and keep you informed of topical financial information.
3. Books – A great way to deepen your financial knowledge and change your financial habits.
4. Provider emails – To keep you updated with new products and ways to save money on your bills or insurance policies.
5. Newspapers – A great way to keep up to date with current financial news; you can be sure the information is current and factual.
6. Newsletters – Monthly newsletters are a great resource to keep you up to speed with your finances.
7. Social media – Keep up with your finances while having fun, by following a few financial gurus. This can be great if you're short on time.

Now think of ways you can apply this to your life, and you'll be on your way to getting on track with your finances in no time!

CHAPTER 11

GENERATIONAL WEALTH – PASSING ON THE BATON

'Build something that outlives you.'
—ALEXANDER ROSE

When you think about generational wealth you probably think about wealthy household names, mansions, yachts and private institutions. However, this is not exactly true about generational wealth. Building generational wealth is all about building, preserving, and eventually passing on wealth to your future generations – whatever that sum may be.

BUILDING WEALTH – LOOKING FOR OPTIMISTIC OPPORTUNITIES

What's your net worth?

A term often associated with celebrities and famous figures. However, regardless of your wealth status, you should identify your net worth. Too many assets and little debts do little for your credit rating, and too many debts and little assets do little for your net worth. It's the first step to generational wealth planning and it's easy as pie to calculate. First, tally all your assets (houses, cars, jewellery, clothes) then subtract all your liabilities (mortgages, credit cards, loans). The remaining amount leftover is your **net worth**. Yes, it's that simple! Once you've established your net worth (net estate value), you can work out if there is any inheritance tax (IHT) to pay (tax paid on the value of your net estate on death) and how much.

> *ASSETS minus LIABILITIES (DEBTS)*
> *= NET WORTH*

It doesn't matter what your net worth is; however, you should aim for your assets list to be longer than your liabilities to help you improve your net worth.

 FOR A PERSONAL VIEW: Have a go at completing the net worth tally (see page 288)

> *Keep working until your ASSETS list*
> *is longer than your LIABILITIES.*

Managing windfalls, winnings and unexpected money
- Have you received a healthy lump sum as a result of an accident or injury?
- Have you been lucky enough to win the lottery?
- Have you played your cards right gambling?

Let's say you've hit the jackpot – hooray! Receiving a money windfall can be an unbelievably life-changing experience. However, it can also be a curse if you're not careful. It may be the first time you have come into such fortune, and therefore you want to ensure you don't blow it all. To avoid this, you want to break down your windfall and think about everything you want to buy first. It may be your dream home, a car, or taking the opportunity to clear all your financial debts – this list may be endless so try to prioritise. After doing this, you will satisfy your financial cravings and feel good.

Next, set a long-term goal for the money. It will enable you to benefit from the money now and in the future. You can achieve this by investing in valuable assets such as property or investments, to drive an income stream or future growth. Finally, try to avoid making significant changes to your monthly budgets, such as leaving your job or careless spending. It could quickly lead you back to where you started, and there may be no money to collect when you pass go!

> *Careless spending could quickly lead you back to where you started, and there may be no money to collect when you pass go!*

If you feel the money you have received is too compelling and challenging for you to control you should get a financial professional involved to help you with planning what to do with it, but other than professionals, you should be careful who you tell about your windfall. The money may make people feel differently about you, but not everyone will be as happy for you. You also want to avoid being the new bank in town. It's perfectly fine to help others and donate your money to those in need, but make sure you list these in your priorities, so you don't lose track of your money by helping others.

Stick to the financial plan you have created, no matter how tempting it can be to spend with abandon. Remember your long-term plans will fund your future desired lifestyle, so don't sell yourself short. Here is a breakdown of the common things you may consider doing with your windfall:

- **Clearing debts** You may choose to pay off debts if the interest rate is higher than you can earn on savings – this is particularly true with credit cards, which can charge double-digit interest rates.

- **Paying down on the mortgage** You may be tempted to pay off a lump sum on your mortgage. However, before pursuing this option, consider eliminating as much as you can of any debt with high interest rates as mortgage interest is usually considerably lower. You should also think before clearing debts on interest-only mortgages or repayment mortgages in the earlier years as the majority of your money will go on interest instead of reducing the much-needed capital.

- **Saving** If you have no emergency funds, it's worth setting aside at least three months' worth of income before you explore other options. For other savings amounts, explore how long you wish to keep the money and compare this to the interest you will receive. If you have no short-term plans for the money, you should avoid holding large sums in savings as the value can decrease over time.

- **Investing** If you have a long-term goal and want to achieve growth or income on your lump sum, you may consider investing it, and if there is a trust involved there may be a requirement to invest. Investing provides the benefit of exploring more tax-efficient advantages compared to savings. You may not be open to risk and that's okay – with careful planning and expert advice you can benefit from long-term potential growth and risk you are comfortable with.

- **Pensions** Depending on your age, investing for retirement may either seem highly attractive or extremely off-putting; generally, the younger you are, the less attractive this option may seem, and you may wish to consider clearing debts, savings or investments before exploring a pension. However, there are still major advantages to benefit from, so don't ignore this option completely (see page 217). Depending on the amount received, pensions may not be the best fit for all the money due to annual allowance restrictions (see page 236).

- **Starting a business** You may have some bright business ideas you want to put into practice, and the lump sum couldn't have come at a better time. However, before plunging in, ensure you put in place a business plan to check the viability of your ideas. Never chuck large sums of money into a business idea or venture without due diligence!
- **Personal treat** You have earned your winnings so enjoy them; go and treat yourself to that fancy sports car or a luxury holiday. Just be sensible and consider some of the above before splashing out.
- **Charity** Giving to charity will make you feel good and fulfilled; another bonus is that your donation can also benefit from tax advantages depending on the charity and amount you gift. Before you gift, you should ensure that you are financially on track.

> *'The greatest thing money can buy is financial freedom.'*
> —DAMIEN THOMAS

WHAT WOULD YOU DO?

Let's say you win £100,000 on the lottery. On the next page are three examples of how three different people used the money.

• Saves £10,000 to cover emergency funds • Uses £10,000 to clear all debts • Pays down £20,000 on the mortgage to reduce the rate • Invests £20,000 into an employer's pension scheme • Invests £20,000 in an ISA • Uses £10,000 to start a side business • Uses £5,000 to upgrade car to a new model • Donates £5,000 to charity	• Saves £5,000 to cover emergency funds • Uses £20,000 to clear some debts • Spends £50,000 on a brand-new car • Spends £10,000 on clothes, shoes and luxury items • Shares £10,000 with family and friends • Considers investing but doesn't proceed • Spends £5,000 on a holiday to Ibiza	• Makes no contribution to saving (already has some emergency funds) • Uses £80,000 as a deposit for a BTL property • Uses £10,000 for renovations to increase rental income • Puts £10,000 aside in a savings account for short-term plans

Your breakdown may look very different if you receive an unexpected lump sum. The point is to plan your money down to the last pound to ensure you get the most benefit. Do any closely mirror what you would do if you received a lump sum of £100,000?

What would you do if you received £100,000 today? Try to list your top five things.

----

*The journey to financial freedom is
different for everyone – stay in your lane!*

PRESERVING WEALTH –
PROTECTING YOUR ASSETS

Leave a legacy for your family – not the taxman!

The notable wealth mogul Warren Buffett is often quoted as saying: 'Someone is sitting in the shade today because someone else planted a tree a long time ago.' You too can pass on the baton of wealth and ensure it remains within your family – there's little point in working hard throughout life without being able to pass it on. Protecting and retaining your wealth can be achieved with careful planning, and you will be pleased to know it can be simple and extremely cost-effective. You should always seek professional legal advice to ensure your plans are suitable as they can easily go wrong when you least expect.

INHERITANCE TAX PLANNING – DON'T GET CAUGHT OUT!

Inheritance tax, generational wealth or legacy planning was once the preserve of the rich and wealthy. However, the rise in property prices over the last few decades and the decrease of the nil rate band has pushed many into the 'rich' bracket. You may not feel you're living a luxury lifestyle, but that doesn't mean you're not asset-rich. Inheritance tax (IHT) is unofficially one of the most hated tax and you may be with the majority in thinking it's unfair to be taxed on wealth built up over one's lifetime. However, with careful planning it is one of the only taxes you can reduce (or get rid of completely), meaning you can relax and leave your assets to your heirs – but you must plan! You have the power to choose from an array of methods to drive down inheritance tax

– helping you to legally save up to hundreds and thousands of pounds. Each person has an allowance of up to £325,000 (£650,000 for married couples) free of inheritance tax, technically known as the nil rate band; anything above is subject to 40% tax.

£1 million residency reducer

Suppose you plan on leaving your main home to your children. In that case, you could benefit from Residence Nil Rate Band (RNRB), an additional nil rate band introduced in 2017 that allows an additional increase of £175,000 to your nil rate band (£325,000). This means that if you are married, you could gift your main residence and pay no inheritance tax up to £1 million (£325,000 + £175,000 x 2). The additional allowance is only available on the main residence and is not applicable for other properties. The following exclusions also apply:

- Properties above £2.4 million (properties above £2 million will have their allowance reduced by £2 for every £1 above; if the value of the property is £2.4 million or above the relief will be lost entirely).
- Unmarried couples will only benefit from half of the RNRB.
- Only children, stepchildren, foster children, grandchildren or children under guardianship can benefit – anyone else is exempt.

On the next page is an example of how inheritance tax may be applied.

	WITHOUT RESIDENCY RELIEF	WITH RESIDENCY RELIEF
Assets	£500,000	£500,000 (£400,000 residential property value)
Liabilities	£100,000	£100,000
Net worth (net estate)	£400,000	£400,000
Nil rate band (NRB)	-£325,000 (not eligible for RNRB)	-£325,000 (NRB) -£175,000 (RNRB)
Taxable amount	£75,000 (net estate minus NRB)	-£100,000 (net estate minus NRB and RNRB)
IHT tax (40%)	£30,000 liability (40% of £75,000)	No IHT to pay

Note that IHT allowances and tax are based on 22/23 and are subject to change in the future and may be different depending on your jurisdiction.

* The following figures, including nil rate band, tax-efficient allowance, tax and qualifying criteria, are subject to future changes.

* The IHT figures provided are for general guidance, and you should seek financial advice for personal recommendations.

> *You may not feel you're living a luxury lifestyle, but that doesn't mean you're not asset-rich.*

WHAT'S THE POINT?

You may think why bother, as you won't be around when it's applied. But organising your estate will mean less money to the taxman and more to your loved ones. Secondly, it is unlikely that your heirs will be able to access your estate unless the inheritance tax is paid, and if they don't, you may end up pouring all your years of hard work down the drain. So, ask yourself, can you afford not to do anything? It's not the most compelling thing to do, and I'm sure you could think of a million other things that tickle your fancy. However, the earlier you address any IHT liabilities, the easier it is to put an effective solution in place. Too often, people fail to address IHT because they may not understand their options and feel it will be too complex. There are a variety of options available, and therefore it is likely there will be one to suit you regardless of your needs and circumstances – so explore them all.

The importance of making a will

A will is the foundation to IHT planning, a legally binding document that expresses your wishes on your death. It can be as simple or complex as you make it. However, in most cases, the point is to ensure your assets go to your spouse or children in the event of a death. It is important to make a will, especially if you have children. It may be something you've been putting off or it may seem like an overwhelming process, which is why, according to many reports, 60% of people in the UK don't have a will. But it is the first and easiest step to getting your estate in order and setting a legacy plan for your future heirs. You must choose an executor, who is the person who will look after your financial affairs and act upon your wishes upon death. It goes without saying this should be someone you trust completely. Ideally, you should select two executors to be on the safe side. Having a will in place ensures your money and assets go to the right people at the right time, and helps you avoid the rules of intestacy (see below).

Once you have put a will in place, you should ensure it remains updated, especially if your financial circumstances change. It's very common to put off making a will with the intention of 'getting round to it', but sometimes, that's too late, so if you're the type to 'put-off' things, mend your ways and get one done as soon as possible.

WHAT HAPPENS IF I DIE WITHOUT A WILL?

If there is no will in place, matters are dealt with under the rules of intestacy, which means the government will decide who will inherit the estate. The result is that your heir or heirs will have little control over how your wealth is distributed. The following flow chart gives you an idea of who will benefit from your estate if you have no will (subject to future changes).

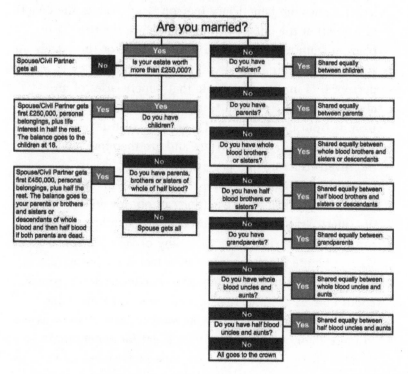

Trusts and transfers

A trust is a legal agreement to transfer wealth such as cash, investment, land or property to someone else, in most cases children. You will need to select trustees (controllers) who will act on your wishes on behalf of the beneficiaries (receivers). Some trusts will also allow you to be a trustee if you want to retain some control, although it is wise to select more than one trustee. You may want to consider trusts if you have more complex needs,

such as leaving assets to someone other than your immediate
family, or if you have a large IHT liability you want to reduce.
There are various trusts, although there are typically two types
of trusts most consider:

- **Absolute trust** Also known as a bare trust, is an
  arrangement whereby a settlor (person who sets up the
  trust) names the beneficiary (person who receives the benefit
  of a trust) at the outset on the deed. Once the trust is in
  place, it cannot be changed at a future date or time. They are
  suitable if you are certain you wish to leave money to one
  person. It is important to note that beneficiaries of an
  absolute trust are entitled to the trust fund and any income
  from it from the age of 18. These types of trust are classed
  as potentially exempt transfers and are therefore subject to
  the seven-year rule (see page 201).
- **Discretionary trust** This allows the option for no named
  beneficiaries. Instead, the settlor can opt for a class or group
  of beneficiaries, such as children or grandchildren, which
  can then be distributed to all or any of your beneficiaries by
  your appointed trustees when they feel it is appropriate.
  You give the trustees the power to make certain decisions
  about how to use the trust income, and sometimes the
  capital. They are suitable if you want to leave cash or assets
  to more than one person and are great for generational
  wealth. These types of trust are classed as chargeable
  lifetime transfers (see page 202).

There are various types of trusts and the details provided are
non-exhaustive. It is wise to get advice on the most suitable trust
to meet your needs and tax efficiency.

Other things to consider
LIFE INSURANCE

It is vital to ensure your life insurances are arranged in trust to help prevent the proceeds of the insurance from being added to your estate, which can cause additional tax problems – especially if held in a sole name. This should be done at the point of taking out the insurance; however, if you have an insurance policy with no trust in place you can contact your existing provider and complete a trust form.

PENSIONS

If you have a pension, you should nominate your beneficiaries by having an Expression of Wishes or Asset Preservation Trust in place. It's a simple document you complete to ensure your pension benefits go to the right people (in most cases your spouse or children) on your death. There is also no cost, so there are no excuses for not having one in place. However, it is not legally binding, so you should still make a will that includes your pension wishes.

POWER OF ATTORNEY

Have you thought about what would happen if you lost mental or physical capacity? How would you continue to manage your financial affairs or personal wellbeing effectively? If you are short of solid answers, then you should consider putting a power of attorney in place if you haven't done so already. A power of attorney is a legal document that allows someone you trust to make important decisions on your behalf. There are two elements:

- **Finances** – includes accessing your accounts, running your business, managing your finances, or even selling your home.
- **Health** – includes helping decide on the right medical care in times of need.

THE SPEEDY SOLUTION TO ESTATE PLANNING

You may find IHT planning overwhelming or perhaps you are seeking a quick-fix solution. Life insurance may be a simple answer to your problems. It is widely used to cover the cost of inheritance tax and can be arranged in trust to your beneficiaries for the IHT amount liable. It is particularly useful if you want to remain in control of your estate, fail to do any inheritance tax plans or to use as a buffer until you put a more effective solution in place. For example, if you have an IHT liability of £200,000, instead of trust options, you may consider a life insurance plan to cover the liability. It's extremely attractive if you are restricted for solutions or other options have proven costly. It is worth noting, however, that protection does not reduce the tax; instead, it ensures the right money is there at the right time. These types of protection can be costly, but if you have sufficient income, it may not be a bad option.

WEALTH TRANSITION

Asset ownership is a great way to pass on wealth for your future generations. Whether you're releasing equity from a property, selling it or gifting money or assets, you want to ensure you transfer your wealth with little tax and protect your hard-earned possessions.

Releasing equity from your home

You may be considering releasing equity or moving your mortgage to another provider, known as a remortgage. People remortgage for various reasons; here are some of the most common ones:

- **Deal ends** When your mortgage product agreement is coming to an end, you'll be moved to what is known as the standard variable rate (SVR), generally much higher than your original deal. You should avoid this at all costs by securing a new rate at least three months before the deal comes to an end (unless the new deals are less favourable than the variable rate). Too often this is overlooked, and people end up paying significantly more – sometimes hundreds of pounds extra.

- **Better deal** You may find a mortgage with a lower rate than your current one, and so it seems like a no-brainer to remortgage. However, you should ensure you explore all the costs involved and search the market to attain the best deal, to save you money.

- **Flexibility** You may find a mortgage with a more flexible deal as not all mortgages allow overpayments or payment holidays (a temporary break from paying or reduced payments for a set period). You may have decided to change from an interest-only mortgage to a repayment one, but your current provider charges a much higher fee or makes the process difficult. If these are important considerations for you, it can be well worth switching.

- **Home improvements** If your home's value has increased, you may wish to free up some of the equity built up in your property; for an extension, to fund home improvements or to buy a second property. You may be able to bag a better deal if interest rates are low, or if your loan-to-value has reduced as a result of your property increasing in value. If you're lucky to find a better deal, you could borrow more money and pay little difference or less than you're currently paying, which would be an amazing result!

- **Consolidate debt** You might want to consolidate debts with high interest to reduce your monthly outgoings, preferring to borrow from the mortgage because it works out cheaper.

- **Change lender** You may have experienced poor service from your mortgage provider and want to change to one with a better reputation for customer service and satisfaction. Conversely, you may want to change to a high street lender as your credit has improved since you originally took out your mortgage. However, if these are the only reasons, try speaking with your lender first; they may be able to resolve any issues and compensate you for any faults or offer more favourable deals in return for your loyalty.

You may wish to remortgage for a combination of the above reasons, but remember to explore all the fine print and seek advice where needed to avoid leaving one bad ship for another.

Selling property

You may need to sell a property to release equity or reduce tax but selling or moving home can be just as stressful as buying or renting, so making the right choices will help alleviate some of those worries. Below shows the process that you should follow to successfully sell your property.

FIND AN ESTATE AGENT When selling a property, a good estate agent can help minimise your fears and maximise results. A poor estate agent will put all your plans on hold, and you will have little control in making changes, so choosing the right one is key. You can look online for an estate agent or get a recommendation to help with a reputable one. Note that if you decide on multiple agents advertising your property, you may end up paying more than one fee. Agents will often charge a percentage, usually 1.5–3% of the property value (costs may vary depending on the estate agent), or a flat rate, so negotiate the best price! You will also need to pay for a home information pack, which includes essential information about the property for the buyer. These cost between £250 and £500

SET AN ASKING PRICE We are often bombarded with conflicting reports on house prices and sometimes it can be hard to know what to believe. Online sites will advertise current property prices; however, this may be quite different from the actual selling price. Discuss and agree with the estate agent and stick to an agreed amount or get a surveyor to value the property.

SELECT A BUYER Once you finally have offers on the table – which can be a speedy process for some and long-winded for others – you need to weigh up the most reliable buyer. Chain-free buyers (with no property to sell) are ideal if you want a simple, straightforward sale. Cash buyers are also great as they don't need to wait for a mortgage to be approved, as are buyers with higher deposits as they are likely to be more serious. Your estate agent will explore all potential buyers and help with the selection process.

OTHER THINGS TO CONSIDER

Other than giving your property a good makeover to make it attractive to potential buyers you need to think about the following:

- **Timescale** You cannot fix a date that you will sell, and chances are you won't sell as quickly as you hoped, but don't be too disheartened. Set a timescale that gives plenty of room for delays, or think of a plan B. If space is an issue, you could consider an extension instead, or if it's additional income you need, think about renting out a room. The point is to remain positive!
- **Tax** You will be subject to capital gains tax (see page 271) if the property you sell is not your main home. So, it's crucial to factor in the tax before the sale, especially if you wish to use your profit to buy another property. However, selling a property can be a great way to significantly reduce IHT (if you plan on spending the money).
- **Surplus money** After the sale you may be left with some extra cash, especially if you are downsizing. Aim to set a plan for the money to ensure you make the best use of your hard-earned profits.

> *It's not about how much money you make,*
> *but how you keep it, make it work hard*
> *and pass it on.*

5 WAYS TO REDUCE YOUR IHT LIABILITY

Investing
THE BENEFITS OF DOING GOOD DEEDS
There is something about giving back and helping others that makes us feel good. But there is also a bonus to reducing your inheritance tax if you gift the right amount. Under the current rules, if you gift 10% or more of your net value estate to a charity, you could reduce your inheritance tax liability from 40% to 36%. You can gift during your lifetime or by noting in your will that you would like a proportion of your estate to go to charity, referred to as charitable legacy. When gifting money to a charity, you should be mindful that a reduced amount of the estate will be left to your heirs (if any).

UTILISING INVESTMENTS
There are some investments you can consider to help reduce IHT, such as the Enterprise Investment Scheme (EIS). This is where you invest in small companies seeking to raise capital and to reward you for investing the government provides a generous 30% tax relief. Also, the amount you invest is exempt from IHT after two years. Sounds too good to be true! Well, these investments are more for sophisticated investors who are willing to take on high risk and therefore may not be suitable for everyone.

Investment bonds are another option to help reduce IHT as they allow you to take tax-deferred withdrawals, which you can choose to spend or gift, conclusively reducing your estate over time.

---

* The following investment figures, including tax-efficient status and qualifying criteria, are subject to future changes.

* The investment information provided is for general guidance, and you should seek financial advice for personal recommendations.

* Investments such as Enterprise Investment Schemes (EISs) and investments bonds carry risk; the value of your money can go up and down, and you could get back less than you initially invested.

Gifting
USING GIFTS TO REDUCE IHT
Gifting while you are still alive is a great way to reduce IHT. However, not all gifts you make will be free; your gifts will be classed as a potentially exempt transfer or a chargeable lifetime transfer for IHT purposes.

Potentially exempt transfer (PET)
This is a gift or transfer of unlimited value, which has the potential to be exempt if you survive seven years from the date of the gift. If you don't survive the gift by seven years, the PET becomes potentially chargeable and is added to the value of your estate for IHT. If the combined value is more than the IHT threshold, IHT may be due. This means the remainder of the gift that falls outside the nil rate band will only be subject to inheritance tax. However, it may benefit from a reduction in tax depending on the number of years the individual survived since the gift. If a death occurs within seven years of the gift, the tax would be as follows:

TIME OF GIFT	REDUCTION IN TAX
Less than 3 years	0%
3–4 years	20%
4–5 years	40%
5–6 years	60%
6–7 years	80%
7 years and above	100%

For example: Shaun gifts a property (mortgage-free) to his son Charlie. The value of the home is £425,000. As it is not his main residence it will not benefit from residency relief. The property is £100,000 above the nil rate band (£325,000) and therefore Shaun must survive seven years to ensure this gift is not subject to IHT. However, Shaun died five years after gifting the property to Charlie. Therefore, the gift was called back into his estate for IHT purposes. Due to the potentially exempt transfer he did not incur the full tax charge of £40,000 (40% of £100,000). Instead, Charlie paid £24,000 (60% off the full IHT rate taxable) on the gift.

Chargeable lifetime transfer (CLT)
A CLT is a gift made during an individual's lifetime that is immediately chargeable to IHT. This does not necessarily mean there will be IHT to pay, but it does have to be assessed to see if a charge to IHT will arise. If the amount gifted is within the available nil rate band, there will be no IHT due immediately. Gifts above the nil rate band will likely suffer a charge of half of the IHT tax rate.

You should seek legal or financial advice on gifts to see what tax implication you may incur, if any.

MAKING USE OF FREE GIFTS
We all love a freebie! And there are plenty of free gifts you can make to help reduce your estate value, if needed, and ultimately reduce or avoid inheritance tax.

Small gifts	£250 can be gifted to as many individuals or trusts as you like within a tax year. It cannot be combined with other exempt gifts, like the annual gift (see below) you have made to someone within the annual exemption year.
Annual gift	You can gift £3,000 per year with no worry of tax, and if you don't use your previous year's allowance personal exemption, then you can gift £6,000. It's an easy and simple way to gift and can be great for gifting to grandchildren.

Wedding gift	Up to £5,000 can be given as a gift from each parent of the married couple. Grandparents can give £2,500, £2,500 can be given from the bridegroom and up to £1,000 from anyone else.
Normal expenditure	One of the most underused exemptions is gifts from income or reasonable expenditure. It's an advantageous exemption because it has no capital limit (subject to HMRC rules), it can be gifted from salary or pension income and it won't count towards IHT. For example, a grandparent who uses their pension income to supplement their grandchild's private school fees.
Charity or political parties	There is zero tax to pay on gifts to UK registered charities, national museums, the National Trust, universities or political parties, so if any are close to your heart it can be a great way to gift at no cost.

* The following figures, including gifts, potential exemptions on transfers, tax-efficient status, tax and qualifying criteria, are subject to future changes.

* The figures provided are for general guidance, and you should seek financial advice for personal recommendations.

* Some gifts may require a survival term beyond seven years and therefore you should seek professional advice where needed.

CHAPTER SUMMARY

List three things you are proud you have accomplished after reading this chapter.

1.

2.

3.

Now list three things you will look forward to doing differently after reading this chapter.

1.

2.

3.

What one thing in this chapter inspired you to change the way you think and feel?

Generational Wealth: signs and signals

Here are five signals to help you stay **on track** and five signs to prevent you falling **off track**.

ON TRACK if you	OFF TRACK if you
Make a will	Fail to make a will when needed
Discover your net worth	Fail to keep track of net worth and improve
Seek advice on any inheritance tax issues	Avoid putting an inheritance tax plan in place
Understand your children's wants – instead of guessing	Only have one executor/trustee
Have a safe place for all your financial information	Have not put life insurances and pensions in trust – they are free so no excuses!

A LETTER TO MY FUTURE SELF

You may feel like you're the only one who goes through financial struggles, but you're not alone, I promise you. Many people just like you are working towards financial success; some have even become successful. So, what is stopping you from achieving the same? It may feel like you'll be living from pay cheque to pay cheque for ever, and you're in a place you cannot escape from. But I'm here to tell you that this will change one day if you put the work in. Who is responsible for this change? You got it; it's you! With the right financial knowledge, confidence, planning and application, you can achieve your financial goals and free yourself from financial burden. You can achieve so much, and you have given yourself a head start by reading this book.

Try writing a letter to your future self. Make a note of all the things you expect to be, your beliefs, values and aspirations, and don't forget to note the things you will no longer accept or poor habits you wish to eliminate. Here's my letter:

Dear Makala (aka Missy)

Right now, I know you think your dreams are unachievable. But I want you to know you can achieve anything you put your mind to, and many people feel the same way you do. What some people show they have is not always what they possess, so stay in your lane and keep striving for success. Your time will come with hard work, dedication and, most of all, belief in yourself. Many people have tried to limit your beliefs, but this is because they usually have low self-esteem and are going through limiting beliefs themselves. At the moment, you may feel like giving up on your dreams. My advice to you is to continue aiming high and reaching for the stars. The sky is the limit for you!

Very soon, you're going to meet people that admire your struggle for greatness and your drive to make a difference and they're going to change your life. Their ambition and dreams will align with yours, and they will inspire you to continue on your journey. And that's just the start, so don't give up now!

You're going to meet a man who makes you really happy and whole inside, and his name is Alex. You will get married, and both own a home one day, and you will bear beautiful children, starting with two adorable girls, Ire and Teni. And, as if that wasn't incredible enough, you're going to find out the most amazing surprise.

You will go on to become the first Black female chartered financial planner in the UK, and after years of experience, you will go on to write a book to financially empower many other individuals – because if you can do it, anyone can.

And for the girl who dropped out of college, you will continue to break barriers, setting a path for many to follow, and have an amazing community of supportive people who will continue to inspire you to do more.

So, keep on going: the road may not be smooth, but the journey will certainly be worth it in the end, I promise! Everything will work out just as planned, or maybe even better!

Lots of love and blessings
Makala Green
xx

Now it's your turn (no holding back!):

Dear future me _____

_____

_____

_____

_____

_____

_____

_____

PART 4

THE FINANCIAL DESTINATION

You may dream about the day you finally stop working, but have you thought about how and when it will happen? If you're serious about living off the fruits of your labour, you need to work at it. If you have spent more hours planning a holiday than you have for your retirement you need to continue reading this book. Many people put off retirement planning until it's too late – do yourself some justice and avoid this if you can. You want to start planning as early as possible so you can comfortably enjoy the lifestyle you desire at your final destination – retirement.

DIRECT YOUR DREAM RETIREMENT

> *Retirement is not the end of the road,*
> *it's the beginning of an open highway.*

We have explored every aspect of financial planning, from budgeting to buying a home; now it's time to direct your dream retirement. Many people have misconceptions about retirement. Unfortunately, this can lead to a lack of planning, meaning you settle for less than you deserve. Step 1 will help you get things into perspective, so you have a clear idea of what you want and need in retirement.

Will I ever retire?

This is an often-asked question. You may feel you'll never save enough for your retirement, mainly because society tends to feed us so much negative information about when and how you can do it successfully. This could well be the reason you haven't started. The reality is, you're not alone, so whether you're keen or in denial, the answer is YES! The sooner you start planning, the better your chances of making the most of your retirement years.

How much should I save towards retirement?

The million-pound question that everyone wants to know. The truth is we are all guilty of not contributing enough towards our retirement. Pensions can be confusing and unattractive – but they really don't have to be. A pension is similar to any other type of saving, so don't treat it any differently.

Start by envisaging your ideal retirement, the age you want to retire and the income you desire, then work backwards to see what you should be saving. If you want a 'boujee' lifestyle in retirement, you will need 'boujee' contributions to build one, and the earlier you start contributing the better. As hard as it may feel to get started your future self will thank you. Even if you start with £5 a day (average £150 per month), this could equate to £10,900* in five years, based on good market conditions. Everyone's income needs in retirement will be different, so take the time to understand your retirement requirements.

*Based on the HSBC investment calculator. It is important to note, the value of your investment can go up or down, and you may get back less than you invested.

Set retirement goals

You may struggle to envisage what retirement looks like for you, especially if it is a long time away, but having an idea of what you'd like retirement to look like will help you build an effective plan. If you're married or have a partner, share your thoughts with them. If you have different expectations about the way you want to live in retirement, it's better to find out now, while you still have time to adjust your plans. List your three retirement goals below in order of priority.

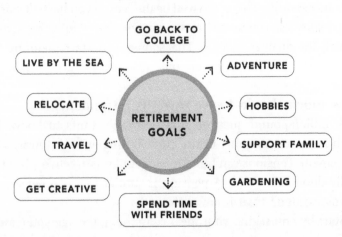

DREAM RETIREMENT PLAN

Who doesn't want to stop working at some point, with all their expenses paid for? Use these pages to map out your ultimate dream retirement, whether that involves cosy staycations at home or jetting abroad to exotic beach locations. The journey to retirement will be different for everyone, but according to the Pensions and Lifetime Savings Association, there are three types of retirement people may have in mind.

MINIMUM Covers basic standard of living with some money left over for fun. This would cover basic needs as well as an annual UK staycation holiday and regular leisure activities. On average a single person will need £10,200 and a couple £15,700 per annum.

MODERATE Provides more financial security and flexibility to live a little. This is likely to cover your standard of living, an annual holiday abroad and money for regular discretionary expenses such as eating out. A single person would need £20,200 and a couple £29,100.

COMFORTABLE This allows you to live a more luxurious lifestyle where you have more control and money to do what you enjoy. This includes multiple trips worldwide, regular beauty treatments, eating out regularly and enjoying a social life including theatre trips. A single person would need £33,000 and a couple £47,500.

It doesn't matter if you cannot achieve your dream retirement but setting the goal and visualising your future retirement is a great way to start or get on track with your retirement journey. Where would you like to live if money was no option? What hobbies would you pursue if you had no trouble with time? Go ahead and allow yourself to indulge your future self – the truth is it's likely to be similar to the life you enjoy today.

Fill in your retirement dreams and plans here to get started:

Where is your dream retirement destination?

Who would be included in your dream retirement?

What are your retirement must-haves?

What things do you want to avoid in retirement?

What is your ideal retirement income?

What is your ideal retirement age?

Think of some things you can do now that will allow you to comfortably retire.

1.

2.

3.

> *Saving for retirement might be HARD,*
> *but retiring with no or little money*
> *is even HARDER*

Planning for retirement through the decades
HOW TO WORK OUT WHAT YOU NEED

Gone are the days when retirement is spent rocking in an armchair, watching the days go by. Things have drastically changed, and people are more adventurous with their retirement plans. Preparing for retirement at any age requires you to estimate your annual expenditure, including essential and non-essential expenses, and the number of years your retirement will last. It's up to you to decide what constitutes an early retirement but if you plan to retire at 60 and hope to live to 90, your retirement will last 30 years. Multiply your annual expenditure by the number of planned retired years. For example, if your expenses are £20,000 per year and you anticipate 30 years in retirement, you would multiply £20,000 by 30, which equates to £600,000 (your ideal pension pot sum). A retirement calculator will help you calculate your needs in retirement, as well as factor in inflation (usually 2% per year) and your investment rate of return (usually an average of 5% projected return). Once you have estimated your retirement cost, subtract any lump sum already built up from existing pensions to find the amount you need to save.

I'm often asked, 'How much do I need to retire on?' It's a question many people struggle with, but I always state, start with the end goal in mind. Once you have a clear picture of how and when you want to retire, you can simply work out how much you need to save. Another good rule of thumb is to have a pension pot worth at least ten times your annual salary by the time you retire. That may sound like a mammoth amount to save. But, like every major challenge, it's about breaking it down into simple steps and starting early will provide ease in later years. It will also increase your chances of building a pension pot that can last the rest of your life.

Here is some useful guidance on planning for a pension in your twenties, thirties, forties and fifties.

In your twenties

Retirement may seem so far off and, you might lack motivation and find it hard to surrender spending now in order to save for the future. But there is nothing better than starting early. Ideally, you should start from your first pay cheque – that's right! If you work for a company, they will enrol you in a workplace pension (subject to eligibility). You can choose to opt out, but it's worth staying in. According to *Which's* pension calculator, if you invest £152 per month into a pension (which averages out at £5 a day) from age 21 to 65 and your employer also matches your monthly contribution, you could end up with an estimated pension pot of £251,576.17, which could provide a non-guaranteed annual income of ££8,317.11 after tax-free cash. (These figures are based on an annual growth rate of 6%, average inflation rate of 2% and annual charges of 0.75%, none of which are guaranteed.)

Ultimately you should aim to have a pension pot equivalent to your annual income by the age of 30. So, if you earn a salary of £35,000, you'll want the value of your retirement savings to be about the same amount. As hard as it may feel to get started, your future self will thank you.

> *If you live fake rich now,*
> *you will retire real broke later.*

In your thirties

You may be tempted to postpone saving for a pension at this time of life – especially if you have children or a mortgage. But if you have the determination to stick to your savings plan, you will have more chance of creating your dream retirement. By the end of your thirties, you should aim to have a pot that's equal to three times your annual salary. As your retirement savings will be locked away for decades, they will have more time to grow without the temptation of accessing your hard-earned savings.

> *Ten years of sacrifice, focus and investing*
> *can set you up for the rest of your life.*

In your forties

Earnings often peak in this decade, allowing you to take advantage of greater financial resources available to you. Can you use your 'fabulous forties' to make bigger strides towards your retirement target? If so, then do! It's the time where pensions should move up on the priority list. Your savings goal should be equal to six times your annual salary by the time you turn 50. However, if you are nowhere near this target that's okay, keep going; every bit counts!

> *'To enjoy a long, comfortable retirement*
> *you need to save more today.'*
> —SUZE ORMAN

In your fifties

Retirement is around the corner, so it's time to make the most of your pension plans. You should get to grips with how much you will need to retire. If you have enough money to live off or if you need to save more and work a bit longer to get there. It's also worth factoring in how much State Pension you could get – every penny counts! Ultimately you should aim to have saved the equivalent of eight times your annual salary by the time you turn 60.

> *'The question isn't at what age I want
> to retire, it's at what income.'*
> —GEORGE FOREMAN

Hit those money milestones and you could set up a solid retirement fund worth multiple times your annual salary as you head
into retirement. Even if you fall far short of these figures don't
feel discouraged; they are simply guides and should only be
considered if you rely solely on pensions to meet your income
needs in retirement. You may wish to include some alternative
options to help you meet your retirement goals (see page 289).
The key is to set a plan that works for you and try your best to
stick with it!

THE BENEFITS OF STARTING

WHAT ARE THE BENEFITS OF A PENSION?

A pension is a vehicle that will provide an income when you decide to stop working, which is commonly known as *retirement.* Whether you are an absolute beginner or want to refresh your understanding, here are some valuable pension benefits:

Get your free share

One of the most attractive things about a pension is the tax relief you receive on entering. In other words, free money from the government – who doesn't like something for nothing? The more you earn, the more tax relief you receive. To illustrate, let's suggest you contribute £1,000 towards a pension over a year; you would receive the following depending on your tax band:

- **Basic rate taxpayer** You get 20% tax relief, which means you will only pay £800; the remaining £200 will be paid on your behalf. In most cases this is done automatically for you.
- **Higher rate taxpayer** You get 40% tax relief, which means you will only pay £600; the remaining £400 will be paid on your behalf. The additional 20% tax relief will need to be reclaimed via self-assessment (the first 20% tax relief is reclaimed at source).
- **Additional rate taxpayer** You get 45% tax relief, which means you will only pay £550; the remaining £450 will be paid on your behalf. The additional 25% will need to be reclaimed via self-assessment (the first 20% tax relief is reclaimed at source).

Tax relief applies to all contributions up to the annual allowance limit of £40,000 or capped at 100% of your annual earnings (subject to earnings and thresholds, which can reduce this allowance). If you have no income, the maximum amount you can contribute is £3,600 (figures correct for 2022/2023 and may be subject to change in future).

Tax-free growth

The money that grows in a pension is completely free of tax, so don't be afraid to put in! Your employer will also contribute towards your pension if you opt in. Take any opportunities to boost your income in retirement.

Tax on the way out

The first 25% or a quarter of your pension is tax-free, unlike any other asset you will invest in. The remainder of the pension is taxable and would be treated as income. The good news is there are a variety of exit routes you can consider to help control the income tax when received (see page 254).

* depending on the pension type, different rules may apply.

Pension Income

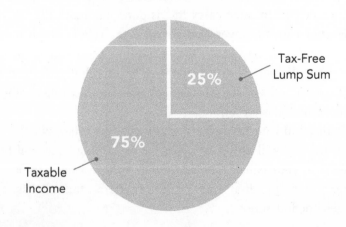

Tax reducer

If you are employed, you have the primary advantage of having your pension deducted before tax, known as a net pension deduction. The more you contribute to your pension, the more you will save in income tax, meaning you pocket more money.

Death benefits

You may be interested to know what will happen to your pension if you die:

- **If you die before age 75** your untouched pension will pass to your nominated beneficiary (chosen person) tax-free, provided it is collected within two years. After that, it will be taxable at the nominated beneficiary income tax rate.
- **If you die after age 75** your untouched pension will pass to your nominated beneficiary, who will pay tax (based on their tax band) on the lump sum or income received.

* depending on the pension type, different rules may apply.

WHY YOU SHOULD PLAN
FOR RETIREMENT EARLY

Saving enough for retirement can strain your budget, especially if you are weighed down by credit card or student loan debt. However, to avoid the inevitable financial shortfall when you choose to retire, you simply can't afford not to plan.

You may be one of many who put off retirement planning and believe you will never retire. But after 30 or 40 years of working, you might feel a little burned out and want to take time for yourself. Even if you consider working beyond 65, the question is, for how long? The truth is there are no guarantees as to how long you will be able to work, so you're better off planning for retirement early, even if you think you might like to continue working beyond. If you need a little more persuading, here are a few other suggestions to plan earlier for your retirement.

Retirement could last longer than you think

We are experiencing a rapid increase in lifespans. People live much longer; according to the Office for National Statistics, in 2020 over 609,503 people were living beyond 90 years old in the UK. For many, retirement is now a long journey to look forward to, not, as it once was, a relatively short one.

The rise of medical advances and public health improvements has resulted in the largest recent increase in centenarians. So, what does this mean for your retirement planning? Put simply: you could spend more than a third of your life in retirement. While this is something to celebrate, you run the risk of outliving your savings without a long-term financial plan. This may bring about worry, but with a structured saving plan in place, you can create a retirement plan that works for you.

The State Pension may not be enough

Most people will get a State Pension, but the income from it alone will probably not cover all your basic needs. If you have not contributed enough years' worth of National Insurance contributions, you will not qualify for the full amount (see www.gov.uk). Suppose you are reliant on state support to meet your needs in retirement; the question might not be how to retire successfully, but when and if at all.

With the anticipated increase in longevity and the declining ratio of those in the workforce compared to those in retirement, the government is proceeding with increasing the State Pension age. The current age is 66 for men and women, increasing to 67 between 2026 and 2028 (see page 224). The Office for Budget Responsibility warned that many people working today may not be eligible for a State Pension until the age of 70, with more expected future changes.

Whatever its future, it's clear that the UK population as a whole may not be able to rely on the State Pension for ever. Therefore, you must take personal responsibility for your retirement finances, as there may be little in the way of the state as a safety net to fall back on.

It can be hard to catch up

A common mistake is to try to play catch-up later on in life. The longer you delay saving, the less time you leave for growth, making it harder to save in future years. The hardship of each pound you save now can be greatly outweighed by the comfort you gain later.

Knowing you'll be all set to maintain your standard of living – with enough left over to let you comfortably do the things you enjoy in retirement – is something well worth striving for. It will also give you far more freedom and control over your lifestyle down the road.

BENEFITS OF RETIREMENT PLANNING

1. You can retire earlier.
2. Less responsibility in later years.
3. Retire with more money.
4. Take control of your retirement.
5. Provide more options to meet retirement goals.

Don't fall into the trap of overestimating your needs

There seems to be little grip on how much retirement income is required and the savings pot needed to translate into sufficient income. According to Money Advice Service (2018) on average, Britons believe that a pot of £233,000 will be enough for their desired retirement income of £26,000 a year. But research suggests that they need to save at least £525,000 for this income, even including the State Pension.

Given increasing life expectancy, it's imperative that we save more to help fund a suitable income in retirement. More than half of people in the UK are either not saving enough or not saving at all for their retirement, to provide the standard of living they envisage.

If this echoes in your ears you have three choices: adjust your income expectations, start saving more, or retire later.

The message is clear: a comfortable retirement can only be assured if you take steps to save enough money and invest wisely. The road to a rewarding retirement is not the same for everyone, but there are plenty of options to choose from, so be sure there will be one to suit your needs.

> *Retirement is not the end of the road, it's the beginning of an open highway.*

PENSION ROUTES

Now you know the benefits of starting a pension it's worth considering your pension options to decide on the right routes for you and your future.

AUTO-ENROLMENT

In April 2016 the government introduced auto-enrolment to encourage more people to save towards retirement; arguably, these now account for the vast majority of workplace pensions with millions enrolled. The employer is obliged to contribute subject to you meeting the eligibility criteria (see www.gov.uk). The amounts contributed are stipulated by the Auto Enrolment rules that set minimum amounts (see page 228), which are subject to annual change. If you are employed, you can contribute more than the minimum and your employer may do the same.

The employer generally sets the retirement age and investment choice. Because of this, your selected investment may be limited if your employer opts for a low-cost pension. You should discuss with your employer to understand if you meet the criteria and how contributing or not will affect you and your pension. If offered a scheme like this, it is wise to opt in because you'll not only be providing towards your retirement but also reducing your monthly tax. Should you decide to start contributing or have already done so, you should explore how you can keep an active check of your pension performance – at least annually. On the other hand, if you opt out of your pension, there is an opportunity to re-enrol once every three years or consider a private pension.

Pensions fall into three broad categories:

1. State Pension
2. Defined Benefit Pension
3. Defined Contribution Pension

STATE PENSION

The State Pension is provided and backed by the government and provides an income you receive at State Pension age, so you don't have to physically contribute. The actual amount you receive is based on National Insurance contributions you pay over your working life. You usually need to have ten qualifying years on your National Insurance record to get anything at all, and a minimum of 35 qualifying years to receive the full State Pension (if you do not have a National Insurance record before 6 April 2016). Even if you are not employed or self-employed, you may still be eligible for qualifying years if you receive certain state benefits, such as carer's allowance, disability allowance and maternity pay.

The State Pension retirement age has increased over the years and is dependent on your date of birth. The current State Pension age is 66 for men and women (for those born after April 1960); there will be a phased increase in State Pension age to 67 (by 2028), and eventually 68 (between 2044 and 2046, subject to life expectancy factors and government changes).

You might get less than the new full State Pension if you were contracted out before 6 April 2016, likewise, if you have gaps in your State Pension or are not on track. However, you have the option to top up or plug any gaps. Go to www.gov.uk/check-state-pension to check your forecast.

Relying on the State Pension only leaves limited options in retirement. Ask yourself whether you could survive on £179.60

per week in retirement (current full basic State Pension in 2021/2022). Probably not! It is unlikely to be enough to support most people's standard of living in retirement, so you must look at all other pension options and alternative routes to enable you to live the lifestyle you deserve.

There are various types of State Pensions, and different rules may apply.

DEFINED BENEFIT PENSION

Often referred to as a workplace pension, this is perceived as the golden pension, also known as the final salary scheme. It offers a guaranteed income for life and is run by employers (sponsors) who give trustees the responsibility to look after the pension on behalf of employees (members). They are highly attractive for their guaranteed income, annual inflation increases and spousal benefits. However, the scheme's rules dictate the age at which you can take benefits – usually 60 or 65 – and therefore, there is little room for flexibility if you want to retire early. Defined benefit schemes are costly for employers to run, making these increasingly rare, so it might be well worth holding on to if you have one. The income benefit you receive is based on three factors:

1. **Salary –** These schemes are generally based on your final salary before retiring or leaving the scheme. However, of late most DB schemes are based on an average salary, normally an average of the last three years before retiring or leaving the scheme.
2. **Length of service –** The number of years you have worked for the employer and contributed to the scheme pension.
3. **Accrual rate –** This is a formula calculated on a fraction of your salary and is normally 1/60th or 1/80th, multiplied by the length of service.

Take a look at this example:

- Final salary before retirement: £30,000
- Length of service: 30 years
- Your company accrual rate: 1/60th.
- Your annual pension: £15,000, calculated as £30,000 (salary) x 30 (years) divided by 60 (accrual rate).

KEY BENEFITS OF DEFINED BENEFIT SCHEMES	KEY DRAWBACKS OF DEFINED BENEFIT SCHEMES
• Guaranteed income • No investment risk • Inflation increases • Spouse and dependant benefits • Protection via the Pension Protection Fund (PPF) if the company becomes insolvent	• Restricting rules • Tax implications • Not advantageous if you have a short life expectancy • Unfavourable death benefits if unmarried, no children or no dependent children • Risk of company insolvency

DEFINED CONTRIBUTION PENSION

This is often referred to as a personal pension and can be under a group scheme or a private one. Defined contribution is based on the theory of what you put in is what you get out, as you build up a pot of money and have the option to choose your income option and the time you take your pension (in line with government guidelines). Unlike DB pension schemes, defined contribution scheme are usually run by a pension company rather than your employer, although your employer may also match your contributions up to a certain limit through an auto-enrolment scheme. Your money is invested into a range of funds, and what you get back in retirement will be based on the size of the fund and the performance of your investment – there are no guarantees.

More employers are increasingly using this pension route to contribute towards employees' pensions, although you can also consider a defined contribution as a personal pension. Whether you contribute with an employer or not, your retirement savings will likely get an extra boost as tax relief is paid on your contributions, with the amount you receive depending on the rate of income tax you pay. Although there are no guarantees on how your fund will perform, one benefit of a DC pension is the flexibility it offers, allowing you to access your savings in several different ways. There are various types of defined contribution schemes that you can consider. Here are some of the common types:

- Personal pension/group personal pension
- Stakeholder pension
- Self-invested personal pension
- Small self-administered scheme

Personal pension/group personal pension

Personal or private pensions are the pensions you set up independently or as a group personal pension (employer scheme). The outcome will be based on the theory 'what you put in is what you get out'. If you actively contribute to a personal pension, you will be gratified with the returns. On the flipside, if you skimp on contributing, you will likely see little value in future. The major advantage of a personal pension is you have complete control over where your money is invested and the age you take your pension (within government and employer rules).

Stakeholder pension

Stakeholder pensions offer a flexible way of saving with minimum contributions and capped charges. They provide a default investment strategy, which can be helpful if you don't want to make investment decisions yourself. It was a common preferred route used by employers to contribute to employees' pensions. However, since the auto-enrolment legislation was introduced in October 2012, employers with five or more staff no longer have to choose a stakeholder pension scheme for them, making these pensions scarce. Stakeholder pensions must meet minimum standards set by the government. These include:

- a legal limit on charges – 1.5% a year of the value of your pension pot in the first ten years, then 1% a year. (But if an employer uses a stakeholder pension to meet their automatic enrolment duties, these are subject to a charge cap of 0.75%.)
- charge-free transfers
- being able to stop or restart contributions at any time, without penalty
- low minimum contributions of no more than £20
- a default investment fund – a ready-made portfolio if you wish to avoid the investment decision.

Self-invested personal pension

A self-invested personal pension (SIPP) is a personal pension with a wide variety of investment options to build up a pot for when you retire. The main difference with a SIPP compared to a personal pension is the flexibility and freedom you have with selecting and managing your investments – hence the term self-invested! Like a personal pension, they can be held as a group workplace scheme by the employer or on a personal basis. SIPPs can offer much wider investment options than other pension types. However, it may require you to have some experience in investing to fully benefit, as you are responsible for your investment choices. The table below shows the assets you can include and those excluded in a SIPP.

INCLUDED	EXCLUDED
Deposit accounts: cash	Residential property
Company shares (recognised UK or overseas)	Commodities
	Overseas unquoted shares
Unit trusts and open-ended investment companies (OEIC)	Loans to members or persons
	Hotel rooms including off-plan hotel developments
Investment trusts	Storage pods
Bonds	
Endowments	
Property and land (for commercial use)	

SIPP charges can often be higher than traditional personal pensions; however, 'low-cost' options with fewer investments are available. Fees might include:

- set-up charges
- ongoing charges figures for the investments
- platform or service charges (to cover the administration of your pension)
- annual administration charges (some providers combine the investment and administration charges)
- dealing fees for investing – with some fees fixed and others percentage-based, depending on the provider

Small self-administered scheme (SSAS)

This is a specialised type of employer-sponsored defined contribution scheme that is set up for a small number of senior staff (often directors or senior executives) with a membership of fewer than 12 employees to build a pension pot. However, they can be open to other workers and even family members.

The primary perk is that all company members can club their pension savings together to create a larger investment pot. The trustees of the scheme generally decide the investment options. They do not benefit from tax relief; instead, all contributions can be claimed back as a tax expense via self-assessment. Additional advantages of a SSAS offer the ability to invest 5% of the total fund value in shares of the company, making an SSAS ideal for directors who require greater control over the pension investments and the ability to borrow from a pension to buy property (commercial). Your entitlement to a SSAS pension when you retire will depend on:

- the amount of money paid in on behalf of that member
- the length of time that each contribution has been invested
- investment growth over this period and the level of charges (if applicable).

* The following pension figures, including retirement ages, tax-efficient status, qualifying criteria, inclusions and exclusions and guarantees are subject to future changes.

* The pension information provided is for general guidance, and you should seek financial advice for personal recommendations.

* Pensions (other than DB schemes) are subject to risk, meaning the value of your money can go up and down, and you could get back less than you initially invested.

CONSOLIDATING AND TRANSFERRING PENSIONS

If you change jobs, go self-employed or have a sudden change in circumstances, you should check your pensions. It is the only way to know whether you're moving in the right direction towards your retirement goal. It's easy to avoid reviewing your retirement needs because you feel it is too complex and most pension statements aren't exactly a relishable read. This section will break down the simple things you need to look out for to maximise your retirement potential. You may have built up several pension pots as a result of changing jobs or careers, which can make it easy to lose track of your pensions. You do have the option to consolidate all your pots, to help you keep track and make your life easier. Consolidating your pensions can offer many advantages, from lower costs to better performance, and easier management, i.e. one statement and payment as opposed to multiple ones. However, consolidating pensions is not always straightforward, and several things need to be taken into consideration before you merge.

Pension treasure hunt!
Check all your pensions, and I mean all of them, including the small pension you may have accrued by working with a company for just a few months. There might be a pension statement you have misplaced, and you can't for the life of you think where to find it, or the pension provider may have changed company. Don't worry; you're not alone. If this is the case, you can trace or track your

misplaced pensions online. If you have multiple pensions, you need to add them all together (see page 300) to get a true income total.

REASONS YOU MIGHT CONSIDER TRANSFERRING YOUR PENSION

Switching your pension is quite different from switching your energy bill. There's a lot to take in, so make sure you weigh up all the pros and cons. The pros could be a higher income or better performance, but whatever your reasons, make sure the options are right for you before you switch. Below are some of the common reasons for transferring.

- **Consolidation** The most common reason why people consider transferring to another provider is to keep everything in one place and avoid confusion.
- **Tax-free lump sum** Some defined benefit schemes may offer less than the government standard (25%) as they are calculated differently due to the guaranteed income they offer, and therefore you might want to get your money's worth. However, this is likely to be at a loss of other benefits, such as dependant's pension or guaranteed income.
- **Flexibility** Your existing pension may be too restrictive, and you may require more freedom. The licence to do what you want with your pension may sound appealing. However, you want to ensure this is not at the risk of you outliving your pension savings, especially if not managed well.
- **Taxation** Some pensions allow you to control the income you receive, which can be tax favourable, particularly if you want to take your income in stages. For example, you may be a high earner and want to gradually take your pension to avoid paying unattractive sums to the taxman.
- **Death benefit** Some pensions offer more flexible options for death benefits, giving you more control over where your

money goes if you die. For example, most defined benefit schemes will determine who your benefits go to – usually a spouse or dependent child (typically up to a maximum age of 18–21). If you are not married or have older children, these death benefits may not be befitting. However, if this is the case, you should consider all other benefits to reassure yourself that it's worth the trouble – if your circumstances change (you marry, remarry or have children), you may give away valuable death benefits.

- **Early retirement** If you are considering retiring early, you'll be rid of working headaches and will receive an income from your pension, and that may sound like an offer you can't refuse. The retirement age on your scheme pension may be well above 55, which can be frustrating if you want to take your pension early. You need a decent-sized pension to retire early – so be sure not to rush into it if you're not ready.

- **Health** Some pensions will offer an increased income if you are in a poor state of health or even if you have a poor lifestyle such as heavy smoking or drinking, so it's worth shopping around to get the best priced annuity (guaranteed income for life). Depending on the severity of your health issues, most schemes will allow you to take benefits early. However, it is wise not to go crazy with your pension in case your health improves.

- **Charges** Feeling that you are being charged more than you bargained for may well be a good reason to switch. Rightfully so, as you could save thousands over time by reducing charges on your pension. However, you may end up paying back the money you save in switching fees, so don't let charges be the determining factor, unless, of course, they are extremely excessive.

CRACKING THE CODE TO YOUR PENSION STATEMENT

Before transferring you should check your pension statements to ensure it makes financial sense. When you look at your pension statement you might think 'What the hell?' This is likely to be the case if you have never checked a statement before or find just the thought of it too overwhelming. Your pension statement may look like a morse code at the moment but don't worry, you are not alone. Here's how to crack the code to your pension statement.

- ✓ **Type of pension** Your pension type, such as **Group Personal Pension, Money Purchase** or **Final Salary,** will be clearly stated on the front page of your pension statement. It gives you a basic insight into what your pension offers. Some may carry strict rules that make it difficult to transfer out, such as defined benefit schemes. Therefore, if you want to compare, you should do so on a like for like basis.
- ✓ **Current value** The value of your pension may be the only thing that grabs your attention on the statement, and sometimes it's the only thing that makes sense. You only need to focus on the current value to see what your pension is worth. If you are looking to transfer your pension, you need to know the **transfer value**, which may differ from the current value, especially for pension schemes that include bonuses. It is important to note most pension providers require you to have a minimum amount in a pension pot before you consider transferring, due to associated costs. You may also be legally required to seek financial advice before transferring any value above £30,000 (defined benefit schemes).
- ✓ **Benefits** Your pension may include complementary or additional benefits in retirement, such as a guaranteed income for life (final salary), which is like gold dust when it comes to benefits. You must understand all the benefits

incorporated in your pension before transferring – if you don't you could lose out!

✓ **Projection** The projection is often found at the back of the statement, which is why it's often missed! It breaks down what your pension will be worth when you retire; in other words, the income you will receive. It is likely to be the part of the statement that stimulates you to save more towards your retirement. It will include the income before tax-free cash, the tax-free cash amount (typically 25% of the pension value) and the income after the tax-free cash (which is likely to be the income you will receive). If you have set a target figure for your retirement, this is the section you should use for comparison.

✓ **Charges** You mainly want to look out for the **Annual Management Charge**, which is the amount it costs to run your pension yearly. It could be found in different places on your pension statement, which may make it difficult to find, but it will be there. If transferring, you should pay close attention to the charges on your current plan in comparison to the proposed pension. If there is little difference, ask yourself: is it worth the hassle?

✓ **Performance** Your pension statement is unlikely to show you how your pension has performed. Instead, it will provide a list of the funds where you are invested. You can use this information to source how your funds or portfolio have performed over the last year, but preferably five years. You can easily check out information on fund performance online (see page 299). It isn't easy to compare your current values, especially if you regularly contribute. However, if your pension value is less than the previous year, that is a sign that it is not performing well and vice versa.

If you are transferring your pension, the performance plays an integral role in the comparison process; however, it should not be the main reason you transfer. You can only assess past performance, which is no guide to the future, and therefore a transfer based on this might not be suitable. Suppose you are not happy with the performance of your existing pension. In that case, you should explore the option to select different funds with your existing provider before considering another.

 PLEASE NOTE: Consolidating pensions is a complex process, and it is highly recommended you seek professional financial advice if you are unsure of your options

Other factors to consider

- **Attitude to risk** Most pensions are exposed to risk, and rightly so to get you the rewards you need in retirement. There is little choice in the risk, but you can control the exposure. Start by selecting a level that suits you: low, medium or high. However, the typical risk profile for the majority of pension investors is medium due to the length of time they are held. As a general guide, the younger you are, the more risk you can afford to take, and the closer you move to your retirement date, the lower your risk will be. Ideally, in the final years before retirement, you should adopt a low-risk strategy.
- **Loss of benefits** When considering a pension switch, you should explore any benefits you will lose and consider any effects it may have in future.
- **Early withdrawal charges** Before transferring, contemplate when you need to take benefits, as early withdrawal charges may apply in the first number of years of starting a pension. Likewise, you may have charges on your existing pension if transferring out.
- **Further contributions** Ask yourself: do you want to continue contributing towards a pension after you take benefits? If so, the tax relief on the amount you contribute may be affected by triggering the Money Purchase Annual Allowance (a reduced annual allowance if taking money from a defined contribution scheme).

ALTERNATIVE RETIREMENT ROUTES

'Retirement is a blank sheet of paper; it is a chance to redesign your life into something new and different.'
—PATRICK FOLEY

ALTERNATIVE OR ADDITIONAL OPTIONS TO PENSIONS

For most people, saving for retirement means contributing as much as possible to a pension, something that many are not prepared or don't feel able to do. A pension has several very important advantages that could make your savings grow more rapidly than they might otherwise elsewhere. With the average retirement now set to last at least two decades, it's important to explore as many incomes as possible to help you build a sufficient pot in retirement. If you're not sure whether a pension is your best option, or you have maximised your pension allowances, here are some alternative options you might consider for your retirement.

1. ISAs

ISAs can complement your pension in several respects; they offer an advantageous alternative if you have maximised your pension allowances, and can provide a flexible tax-efficient income in retirement – especially if you have plans of retiring before the legal pension age (currently 55, subject to future increases). However, funds held in an ISA are not exempt from inheritance tax (IHT) like pensions and may therefore potentially be subject to tax on death.

2. LIFETIME ISA (LISA)

The LISA may be a good choice for retirement savings as it offers bonuses. It can be a great alternative if you have exhausted your pension allowances and cannot benefit from employer's contributions. So, if you are under 40 and fairly certain you will use up your annual pension allowance a LISA could be worthwhile. However, you may still be better off saving for retirement through your workplace pension due to additional contributions from your employer (if available).

3. SAVE AS YOU EARN (SAYE)

SAYE offers you the opportunity to take a direct stake in the company you work for. This is done through a deduction from your monthly salary, and at the end of the term (usually 3–5 years), you can exercise an option to buy company shares back at the original price – usually at a 20% discount on their original value. If the share price falls, you can still get your money back including a tax-free bonus.

If you have the opportunity to contribute to a SAYE scheme, you can transfer the balance of the shares directly into an ISA, provided this is done within a 90-day timeframe, and there is no tax liability. Transfers outside of an ISA may be liable to tax (income tax and capital gains).

4. VENTURE CAPITAL TRUSTS (VCTS) AND ENTERPRISE INVESTMENT SCHEMES (EIS)

These offer attractive growth potential through investing in new start-ups and other companies not typically trading on the stock exchange, not to mention the favourable tax relief offered. However, EIS and VCT investments are only typically suited to experienced or high-net-worth investors willing to take a high-risk approach on investments. With this in mind, it's fair to say these alternatives are not suited to most people's retirement savings.

5. PROPERTY

If you are a property owner, another possible solution is to sell up, release equity or downsize, to fund your retirement. However, you should be mindful that tax and state benefits may be affected. It is worth checking how you would be affected before exploring these options, including factoring in your plans for the property, such as moving out, selling or passing on to future generations.

* The following pension alternative information, including tax-efficient status, qualifying criteria, advantages and disadvantages, are subject to future changes.

* The information provided in this section is for general guidance, before seeking alternative retirement options, and you should seek financial advice for personal recommendations.

* Some alternative retirement options may be subject to risk, meaning the value of your money can go up and down, and you could get back less than you initially invested.

Summary

There are many options you can explore to enjoy your retirement. If you have exhausted your pension allowances, then you may wish to consider other options. The key is balancing the benefits and aligning your retirement portfolio, to coincide with your expected income needs in retirement.

APPROACHING RETIREMENT

> *'Retirement – when you stop living at work*
> *and start working at living.'*
> —DANIELLE DUCKERY

Retirement planning is about planning for the point in life where you throw in the towel and get to enjoy the fruits of your labour. For this reason, it will be different for everyone. The younger you retire, the more active you will be, but a healthier pension pot will be required to last for many years. Conversely, you may leave retirement until your later years, which may be a deliberate choice or through no choice of your own.

Retirement is not necessarily bound by age, but by how much you have contributed towards your pension or other income-producing assets. Deciding when to retire is about deciding whether you can *afford* to retire. The size of your pot will determine how far you can go, whether that's Brighton, Cornwall or the Caribbean. Retirement is what you make it, but with the right knowledge and application, you can achieve one you truly deserve. This section will explore the next steps you need to take to get more benefit from the hard work you've put in over the years.

> **It's time to let go of the TENSION**
> **and enjoy your PENSION!**

POST CAREER PLAN

After working for many years, you're bound to want to retire at some point even if you love what you do. If that point is shortly approaching, it's time to get planning. To enjoy the retirement you genuinely deserve you want to seize the moment – and think about the final preparation. You may have invested in pensions over the years; well, now's the time to review them. If you have never budgeted, then it's a good time to start – you will thank yourself later. You also need to consider other options that could provide an income buffer if needed.

You should explore your options at least a year before you plan to retire. It will give you enough time to work out how much you need, the best route to take and help you map out your desired lifestyle in retirement. Be prepared to consider more than one income option as it is likely no one solution will fit all your retirement needs. In some cases, once you have executed a decision, there is no going back, so be sure to consider all your options beforehand.

GOAL SETTING FOR RETIREMENT

The logical starting point is YOU. How do you envisage retirement? Are you thinking about a world cruise, time with friends and family, or ticking off things on your bucket list? Think about how and where you want to live. Maybe you want to enjoy an annual holiday overseas, or even move to a new country. Your retirement goals will depend on how you spend your working life. You may be used to working long hours or have spent most of your years raising children – probably both. If this is the case, you're likely to want a relaxing retirement where you can focus on things you enjoy.

On the contrary, you may have become accustomed to a busy life and find it difficult to wind down and want to keep very

active in retirement. The main thing is that you map your retirement around your needs and desires. Use the box on page 289
to list your retirement goals and add a price tag to each. You may
be surprised how many things you can do without breaking the
bank.

 FOR A PERSONAL VIEW: Complete retirement goals
planner (see page 289)

DECIDING THE BEST AGE TO RETIRE

The truth is the best age to retire is the age that works for you.
However, it's wise to give this some thought as your retirement
age is only viable based on you having a sustainable income to
last as long as you do – the earlier you retire, the more you will
need. The government enforces a minimum pension age of 55
(related to pensions), which will increase over the years. Some
pensions such as military pensions will pay out before this,
whereas others will range between 60 and 65. However, you can
access most pensions at 55 unless there are restrictions that state
otherwise (common with final salary schemes). If restrictions
apply, you will be forced to comply with the scheme's pension
age, meaning you cannot access your pension unless you have
severe health conditions, or you transfer out.

Realistically speaking, even if you can retire at 55 you may not
have this option, simply because you may not have built up a pot
big enough to maintain your standard of living. It goes without
saying that if this is the case, retiring would be unwise. One
option that is becoming increasingly common is to partially retire,
where you take part of your pension and continue working at
reduced hours. This might be attractive to you if you are used to
being busy and want to continue working with reduced hours.
Your profession may highly value your expertise regardless of

your age, which is common with professions such as doctors, nurses and police officers, and you may extend work with fewer duties. Likewise, you may decide to take on some voluntary work for a local charity that is dear to your heart. If you wish to work beyond your retirement age, you can do so; however, you must decide on your pension options by your 75th birthday.

* The minimum pension age is set to increase to 57 in April 2028 (subject to government changes

HOW MUCH IS ENOUGH?

There is no clear-cut answer as income needs in retirement will be different for everyone and are likely to change during the various stages in retirement. You may plan for more outgoing activities, holidays and helping children in the early years of your retirement, while you may need to consider long-term care when winding down in your later years, so you will need the flexibility to be able to adapt your income to suit your needs, as well as deal with unforeseen circumstances. On the other hand, you may want to live a steady life and might not fancy a lavish lifestyle! If this is the case, you may prefer constant and consistent income that increases over time with the cost of living (inflation), so you can keep pace. The key is planning to ensure your retirement funds work around you and not the other way round. Thinking about whether you have enough to retire can be daunting, but you just need to be realistic with your plans and make sure your needs are in line with what you have tucked away in pensions and other assets. For example, there's no point expecting an annual income of £50,000 in retirement when you've barely contributed to any pensions throughout your working life. Once you have determined the actual income figure you need, decide whether there's enough in the pot to sustain you so that you don't outlive your savings.

Consider the cost of long-term care

Of the many ways you may imagine spending your money in retirement – travelling, enjoying hobbies, helping grandchildren and supporting charities – funding the cost of care is not likely to be at the top of the list. But when considering retirement planning, it would be remiss not to factor in the potential long-term care costs, as these may well be one of the most important expenses. In the UK, the monthly average cost of residential care is £2,816 per month (or £34,000 per year) and receiving nursing care in a care home costs on average £3,552 – which for most people is like paying a triple mortgage. As frightening as it may sound, if your health and mobility are impaired in retirement, you will likely need additional support.

Long-term care may be a significant factor, depending on the level of assistance you need and what support you might have from your family. The cost of care can be as alarming as your future health needs. However, long-term care can be delivered in various ways and there are multiple approaches to paying for it. The cost of care you are required to pay will depend on your assets such as your house, finances and where you live. Therefore, it's a good idea to familiarise yourself with the financial figures and plan ahead. One of the biggest fears about funding long-term care is that you'll be forced to sell your home if you need to move into a care home. However, this is not always the case. For example, if you need care in your own home, its value isn't counted. This is also the case if you move into a care home, but your partner, another dependant, elderly or frail relative continues to live in your own home. You may also be entitled to local council or NHS funding, which will mean your care is state-funded. Alternatively, if you are not eligible for state funding, your care will be self-funded. Here are some of the ways care can be funded.

NHS CONTINUING HEALTHCARE (CHC) This is healthcare arranged and funded by the NHS in England, Northern Ireland and Wales. If you have a disability or complex medical problems, you might qualify for free NHS continuing healthcare (CHC), where care is provided in the home, care home, nursing home or hospice. (Different terms may apply depending on your jurisdiction.)

LOCAL AUTHORITY FUNDING According to research conducted by the Local Government Association, 44% of people think that the NHS provides social care, and 28% think it is free. Your local council might be able to help you with the costs of a care home. Alternatively, you can opt to receive stay-at-home care. The amount of funding will depend on:

- your individual needs – based on care needs assessment.
- how much you can afford to pay towards the costs of care yourself – following a financial assessment.

SELF FUNDING This is where you are not entitled to any funding due to failing to meet funding eligibility criteria. For example, the amount of savings you have may exceed the threshold (see www.gov.uk), meaning you may be responsible for some or all of the care costs. If this happens, you'll need to think about how you're going to top up any contributions or if you have to pay for it all yourself.

Even if you have to pay for care, you might still be entitled to claim some benefits. These benefits aren't means-tested, so you could get them if your health needs are great enough, regardless of your income and savings:

- Attendance Allowance – if you've reached State Pension age.
- Personal Independence Payment (which replaces the Disability Living Allowance) if you're aged 16 or over but under State Pension age.

Hopefully, you can see the importance of factoring in the possibility of funding your long-term care needs, or at least creating a plan of action should the need arise. Here are some of your options:

Income: This could be from your pensions, savings (interest), investments (dividends) or rental income and might be enough to cover some or all care costs.

Savings: This could include money you hold in cash, ISAs or other savings accounts. You'll need to be careful your capital doesn't erode too quickly.

Investments: Investments such as unit trusts, ISAs and investment bonds are the most common options. However, a word of caution: the investments that offer the greatest potential chances of growth usually bear the highest risk, so it's important to strike a balance.

Immediate needs annuities: These are designed to cover any income shortfall to pay for the cost of your care for the rest of your life. You offer a one-off lump sum in return for a guaranteed tax-free income for life, paid directly to the care provider.

Property: Selling your home is one option, but is not always the most convenient. Other options you can consider include:

- Equity release (see page 260).
- Rental income from a property is a great way to cover regular care costs without selling it (see page 116).
- Deferred payment agreement. This arrangement with the local council allows you to get help with paying care home costs. If you qualify, it enables you to receive a loan from your local authority secured against your home. You can delay all repayments until you choose to sell your home or in the event of death. (The debt must be paid, plus interest, within 90 days of death.)

While it's key to understand all of these options, it is important you make the right choices to ensure your care needs and estate are well looked after, as you may have plans to leave some assets to loved ones. It's easy to make the wrong decisions and even risk running out of money, which means you could end up relying on the state. Some may think that's OK, but if it happens you'll end up with limited care choices. So, explore your options well, set your priorities and seek professional advice, so you factor in the worst but focus on enjoying life in retirement.

DIRECT YOUR EXPENSES

The good news is there are some things you have more control over, and that's deciding and directing your income. You may not need as much income as you think in retirement, as you'll likely be cutting back somewhat on your expenditure. However, it's important to understand whether this is the case and if not, how you can rectify it. Get down to the nitty-gritty and decide which expenses will walk their way out, which will make their way in and those that will stay put – down to the last penny. The lifestyle you desire will play a huge factor. For instance, if you're planning on ramping up your social life, you'll need to account for that. It's important to be as accurate and realistic as possible. For example, your utility bills aren't going to go anywhere and indeed may increase the more time you spend at home.

Conversely, the most satisfying part of this planning is looking at the expenses that will retire when you do, such as your mortgage (in an ideal world) and travel expenses if you stop working.

 FOR A PERSONAL VIEW: Refer back to the chapter on budgeting to help you work out your retirement expenses and try completing the How much income will you need in retirement? planner see page 290)

ACCESSING YOUR PENSION POT

> *'Sit back and relax and do the things*
> *you never got a chance to do.'*
> —JULIE HERBERT

Putting the final pieces of your retirement puzzle together can often be the most difficult; there are so many options available that you may feel overwhelmed as to which is best for you. Retiring is a significant life event, and you may be thrilled to bits or dreading it. This section will give you all the knowledge and tips you need to provide peace of mind.

WHERE DO I START?

Life doesn't stop in retirement; in fact, it may be the beginning of a new adventure and an exciting chapter in your life. Therefore, planning is crucial. Start by setting goals (which you should have done after reading the previous steps). Your goal may be as simple as trying not to run out of money in retirement. Contrarily, you may have plans to spend all your money throughout your life. The main point is that your goals will shape the type of income structure you need in retirement.

You may still think you are not ready to retire. Hopefully, this book has provided some comfort so far and at the end will give you a clear idea of your options and the best position to be in. Regardless of how much you've built up, with a robust plan for your future, you could be on your way to a retirement well worth living.

ARE YOU ON TRACK TO RETIRE?

Once you have identified all the income you need and the pensions or retirement options you have, you can quickly work out whether you are on track to retire. If you have achieved the right income, you should be proud of yourself; you did it, all those years of work have finally paid off so let the celebrations begin. If you have discovered you are not on track to retire, don't panic. Have a look at a couple of options you can consider:

1. **Working part-time** It may not be your ideal choice, but it means you can still celebrate a partial retirement and work towards completely retiring. If you explore this route, you should still aim to contribute towards your pension (although restrictions may apply).

2. **Take some tax-free cash and leave the rest invested** You can take your tax-free lump sum and use it to cover the cost of a few retirement goals to give you some satisfaction or to provide an additional income. The rest of your pension will remain invested and can continue to grow.

SIX PRACTICAL WAYS TO MAKE THE MOST OF YOUR PENSION LUMP SUM

The thing that is likely to excite you about retirement is your tax-free cash. Why? Because it's **free** of tax (25% of pension value). It means if you have a pot of £100,000, you can draw £25,000 with no tax to pay. You may be in a hurry to get hold of this money, but it is important to take your time and set a plan (based on your goals). It is the most valuable part of your pension so treat it with care. Here are the various options you can consider for your tax-free cash lump sum.

1. Stash the cash

You may consider keeping your lump sum in cash because it's safe and tax-free if placed in a cash ISA. Sounds like a perfect solution for your tax-free lump sum! However, cash is not ideal for long-term savings because the value can depreciate, especially when interest rates are low. Cash accounts are suitable for emergency funds (ideally six months of expenses), short-term savings and perhaps for the odd extra spend on a day-to-day basis. Avoid keeping excess funds in cash.

ADVANTAGES	DISADVANTAGES
• Your money is safe and secure • Easy to access • Great for the short term • Inherited ISA benefits	• Exposed to inflation risk • Easy to access and spend • Not suited for the long term • Exposed to inheritance tax

2. Investments

You may consider investments, and this can be a great home for your tax-free lump sum. You have an array of tax-efficient investment options such as stocks and shares ISAs, unit trusts (make use of dividend allowances) and investment bonds. The investment structures that will suit you best all depends on how much you are investing and your risk appetite. However, you should avoid exposing your tax-free money to taxable investments as this defeats the objective, therefore, you should aim to maximise your ISA allowance first. Investments are long-term and carry risk, so make sure you are informed before investing.

ADVANTAGES	DISADVANTAGES
• Potential future growth • Opportunities for fixed income • Tax-efficient investments • Ability to reduce inheritance tax	• Capital risk exposure • Money may not be easy to access • Costs and charges may apply • Not suitable for the short term

3. Clear the mortgage and debts

No one wants to retire with debt, and so you may consider using your tax-free cash lump sum to clear your mortgage or other debts. How nice would it be to be debt-free? As lovely as this sounds, you should have good reasons for paying off your mortgage or liabilities with your tax-free lump sum. It may be that you have little income, and the mortgage or debt is unaffordable, or you may have enough funds to allow you to clear it, so it seems like a sensible option. However, you must be certain that clearing debts with your lump sum will not leave you financially disadvantaged in future years. If so, you may consider other options to clear debts, such as extending your mortgage or delaying retiring.

ADVANTAGES	DISADVANTAGES
• Reduce monthly expenses • Debt-free = stress-free • 100% equity in your property • Sense of achievement and peace of mind	• Early repayment charges are tied to some products • Overpayment charges if they are more than the set limit • Potential increase to inheritance tax • If you want to borrow the money back you may be subject to affordability checks to ensure you can afford it

4. Buy a property

You may be thinking of using your tax-free cash lump sum to buy a rental property. It may be the only thing you can think of doing with the money. There is no denying the appealing income benefits that buying property provides. However, it can still have some eye-opening drawbacks, so consider the following, especially if it is your first buy to let purchase.

ADVANTAGES	DISADVANTAGES
• Tangible asset that you can feel and touch • Value-adding opportunity (i.e. renovations) • Regular income through renting • Benefit from property price increases • Keep it in the family by passing down through generations	• Maintenance and repairs can be time-consuming and costly • Property management costs • Additional stamp duty on buy to let purchases • Income tax liability on the rental income • Filing annual tax returns or additional cost of hiring an accountant • Loss of income if tenants fail to pay

5. Supporting family

Before telling your family that you have a lump sum coming your way, remember this is your life savings. You need to plan for YOU first. Whether you're financially supporting your parents, children or an aunt you don't see often, it's essential to explore the best ways to support your family without sacrificing your future. You may feel you haven't had an opportunity before and now's the chance with your retirement money. But you need to be sure before helping others that you have your own house in order. According to the Office for National Statistics the need to support other family generations has impacted one in four people's retirement finances. If you have children, you may feel the financial support is a never-ending cycle. Well, now it's your time, as selfish as that may seem; you have worked hard for the money, and you want to avoid gifting it without proper thought. After all, it's the savings you need to survive on for the rest of your life, so think wisely before gifting away.

> *The need to support other family generations has impacted 1 in 4 people's retirement finances.*

6. Treat yourself

Saving the best till last! Treating yourself is a given and may take first place on your list, and rightly so, but the big question is how much and how often? Depending on who you are and your regular spending habits, this will differ significantly from one person to the next. You may have your eye on the flashy sports car that you can finally afford, or a cruise around the Med. Even if you decide to use most of your lump sum, consider holding back at least a little; there may be other important things you will want in future. At the same time, make sure that while you treat yourself, you don't lose sight of covering your standard of living in later years.

ADVANTAGES	DISADVANTAGES
• Gratifying feeling – makes you feel good	• It's easy to go wild. Make a list and stick to it!
• Avoids feeling resentment in the future	• Depreciating assets such as cars will lose value over time and cost more to replace
• Something to show for your years of work	

The ultimate decision is yours and should not be one you rush into. It's good practice to seek financial advice to ensure your options align with your income needs in retirement and your time restraints; after all, retirement is for enjoying!

ACCESSING THE REMAINDER OF YOUR PENSION POT

The remainder of your pension is taxable; however, there is room for flexibility, and therefore, you should decide on an option right for you.

In April 2015, the government introduced pension freedoms, where anyone of pensionable age will have more freedom and choice about how to access their pensions. The greater choice, however, has left many muddled on the right option to choose to suit their lifestyle, work and leisure in retirement. You may want to defer taking your pension at your selected retirement age if you have no need for income. Alternatively, you may want to access the whole pot if you're not dependent on the income due to other income-producing assets. This section will help you unlock the uncertainty that surrounds pensions to assist you in making the right decision at the right time.

Don't forget to shop around!

When considering your pension options don't rely on the first income option you are offered as you may be able to receive a higher income by shopping around. You simply can't afford to throw away any money in retirement.

Three avenues to access your pension

ANNUITY

Before pension freedoms, annuities were the only income route in retirement. An annuity is where you trade a lump sum of cash for a guaranteed income for life (lifetime annuity) or a set period (fixed annuity), provided by an insurance company. They are usually offered by your employers' pension scheme when you are ready to retire. Providers' offerings will vary based on levels of income, but ultimately the amount you receive will depend on the size of your pot, your health and lifestyle, the age you retire and even where you live in retirement. To get a competitive annuity rate, you should search the open market, which is simple to do online (see page 300). Below are some of the additional benefits you can select with your annuity. However, any added benefits will likely result in a reduction of income, so choose wisely.

- **Joint/single** Joint annuities will offer less income than a single one.
- **Guaranteed period** Income is guaranteed to continue after death for a set period – typically 5–10 years.
- **Level/escalating (inflation-linked) annuity** Reflects how you require your regular payments to move in future. Level is suitable if you want your income to remain the same for life or a set period. Alternatively, escalating (inflation-linked) is suitable if you require your income to escalate with the cost of living.
- **Value protection** Designed to pay the value of your pot to a nominated beneficiary upon death. It is based on the original annuity amount minus any payments already paid, and therefore the benefit will reduce over time.
- **Enhanced/impaired annuity** If you have poor health or lifestyle such as excessive smoking you may be entitled to a higher income through the enhanced or impaired annuity.

FLEXIBLE INCOME DRAWDOWN

Income drawdown came about as a result of pensioners' disapproval over pension inflexibility. Therefore, the government introduced an option to allow people to spend their life savings in a way that suits them. It allows you to invest your pension pot into an investment to provide income flexibility and growth. You can defer income, take income as and when needed, or take tax-free cash and leave the remainder invested. It is suitable if you have a large pension that you wish to control, aim to continue working beyond retirement age and want to defer your pension or you are not heavily dependent on pensions due to alternative options. You must be aware that income or capital is not guaranteed and is exposed to risk. You have control over where the funds are invested, so choose an investment strategy aligned to your goals or seek advice. If you change your mind or feel a drawdown is no longer suitable, you can switch to an annuity at any time.

UNCRYSTALLISED FUNDS PENSION LUMP SUM (UPFLS)

This is a great option if you want full control of your pension, as it provides the opportunity to take some or all of the pension as a lump sum with no obligation to take an income. Every lump sum withdrawn will have the first 25% tax-free, and the remainder will be taxed (if above personal allowance). For example, if you decide to take £10,000 from your pension as a UPFLS, £2,500 will be tax-free and £7,500 will be taxed as income. UPFLS is great if you need to access all of your pension or do not require income. UPFLS is the least common option of the three – it can offer advantageous access to your pension pot if it meets your requirements but could be an absolute blunder if not, as money left outside a pension can be liable to inheritance tax. It can also affect means-tested benefits, as well as the amount you can contribute further into a pension.

RETIREMENT INCOME COMPARISON			
OPTIONS	ANNUITY	FLEXIBLE DRAW-DOWN	UPFLS
Access to income	✓	✓	✗
Access to lump sums	✗	✓	✓

RETIREMENT INCOME COMPARISON			
Guaranteed income	✓	✗	✗
Flexible income	✗	✓	✓
Regular income	✓	✓	✗
25% tax-free cash available	✓	✓	✗
Option to change my mind	✗	✓	✓
Could I run out of money?	✗	✓	✓
Higher income for poor health	✓	✗	✗

Alternative income options

You may feel you haven't built up enough in a pension or have hedged your bets in other assets. Don't worry; retirement planning isn't one-size-fits-all; it comes in many shapes and sizes. The important thing is you arrange something that will offer you a suitable income. By doing so, you'll avoid working longer than expected and will be able to maintain your standard of living when you do retire. There are a variety of options you can consider to meet your income goal or fill an income shortfall.

INVESTMENTS

If you have built up a decent amount in investments, it could work out particularly well if you retire and still have an income shortfall or you require a luxury fund to cover your retirement bucket list. Investments provide more control and flexibility. You have the option of taking what you want when you want, although you should only take the amount you need. Otherwise, there's a risk of your money sitting around doing nothing when it could have been growing.

Another benefit is the tax-reducing opportunities as you can take advantage of tax-efficient investments and allowances. Take ISAs, for example; imagine you had maximised your ISA allowance from inception in 1999. You would have £221,520 saved (in cash ISA between 1999 and 2022). You would have access to draw this money completely tax-free. The disadvantage of solely relying on investments is that you need a large amount in the pot to achieve sufficient income.

PROPERTY

There are various types of rental property: BTL, holiday homes, time share, Airbnb, or even renting a room in your home. Property has proven a good hedge in keeping its value and providing a relatively quick steady income – a match made in heaven for retirement. However, there are still some drawbacks that you should consider before sticking all your money in one property basket (see page 252).

DOWNSIZING – YOUR MAIN HOME

You may be looking for options to make the best use of the equity in your home. As you approach retirement, you may feel you have outgrown your abode, your children have grown and flown the nest, and you find yourself maintaining a house far larger than you need. You may want to downsize and buy a house in the country, or cash in some equity in your property to support your retirement – perhaps a bit of both. Whatever your reasons, it's essential to weigh up all the possibilities.

BUSINESS

I often hear the term 'my business is my pension', which can ring true. Starting or continuing a business in retirement can be an exciting task and keep you busy if you don't like the thought of completely winding down, especially if you operate a business that will continue to provide an income with minimal effort. In this way, you can maintain your standard of living as you enjoy your retired years. However, this option should be taken with caution as there are so many things that can affect your business income: your health, the economy or a pandemic to name a few. Therefore, it's always worthwhile diversifying your income in retirement.

* The following retirement alternatives explore advantages and disadvantages. However, the information is non-exhaustive and there may be other benefits and drawbacks that have not been included in this book. Therefore, you should seek professional advice for personal recommendations.

* Some retirement options carry risk and you should explore all details to ensure it is a suitable option.

WHAT IF?

I still have a mortgage in retirement

If you are approaching retirement and still have a mortgage, don't worry – it's really not the end of the world. There are countless options you can consider to still make the most of your retired years.

- **Extend the mortgage beyond retirement** Many lenders will consider most mortgage terms to the age of 70, and some will even go as far as to age 90. You will need to prove that you can afford the mortgage, which will be assessed on your pension or alternative income in retirement. It may not suit everyone, but it's an option worth considering, giving you additional years to clear the mortgage.
- **Retirement interest-only mortgage (RIO)** If you still have a mortgage in retirement and find it hard to renew by way of a conventional route, or decide to unlock some equity in your home to meet your retirement goals, RIO could be

suitable for you. Unlike your traditional mortgage, you don't have to demonstrate an appropriate payment plan. The added advantage is you don't have to pay the mortgage back until you die, go into long-term care or sell your home. However, it must be paid back, and you will still be accountable for monthly payments, so you must have enough income to afford this option.

- **Equity Release** There are two main types; Lifetime mortgage (borrow money against your home) and Home reversion plan (sell or part of your home). The debt is not repaid until you sell the home, die or permanently move into residential care.

*Equity release reduces your estate's value and may affect means-tested benefits. Therefore, care should be taken before consideration.

Unpredictable factors affect my pension

It's worth noting the factors that may affect your pension, even if they are beyond your control. Here are a few considerations:

- **Tax** If your tax changes, this could affect the income you receive. You should review your overall income and take advantage of tax-efficient options and allowances available to avoid paying oodles in tax.
- **Health and lifestyle** One of the things we cannot predict in life is the state of our health. Depending on the severity, you may need to use significant proportions of your pension to maintain your health. You also have the option to access enhanced and impaired annuities.
- **Recession** If you experience a period of economic decline in your retirement, this is likely to influence how your pension grows or the income you receive (if flexible). The best thing to do is to factor in the likelihood of at least one recession throughout your retirement years, and there are tools available to help you see what things would look like during adverse times.

- **Risk** There are various types of risks you may be susceptible to in retirement, and therefore you should identify them so you can try to avoid some bad roads along the way.

SEQUENCING RISK	LONGEVITY RISK
You may need to draw down on your income when markets are low, which could mean you get less than your money's worth.	People are living longer, and you may live longer than you expect. Centenarian celebrations are becoming the norm, and your retirement years could last just as long as your working years, so plan for this. You want to ensure you have a retirement fund that will outlive you and not the other way around. A useful guide for life expectancy is your family history. Of course, you cannot solely rely on your family heritage as your health and lifestyle are major factors.
CURRENCY RISK	INFLATION RISK
When the currency you use for income is low, and you continue to draw the same value, you could be disadvantaged as you will not be able to buy the same basket of goods, especially if prices increase.	Even with inflation-linked pensions, there is no guarantee your pension will always rise in line with inflation. Therefore, there is a risk your pension funds will not keep pace with the cost of living.

Note: Some of these risks are unavoidable but can be mitigated or reduced with careful planning, including not being reliant on one income source in retirement.

Financial Destination: signs and signals

Here are five signals to help you stay **on track** and five signs to prevent you falling **off track**.

ON TRACK if you	OFF TRACK if you
Start contributing to a pension early	Procrastinate over starting a pension
Set a retirement goal	Fail to contribute enough
Make use of employer incentives such as salary sacrifice	Limit your investment choice
	Opt out of a pension with no plan B
Consider all options before choosing the right pension	Think you will retire comfortably with minimal financial effort

YOUR FINANCIAL CHECKLISTS

WOW! You have arrived at the final financial destination! Hopefully, you are feeling financially empowered and full of confidence to take control of your financial journey and, dare I say, a bit more financially savvy. I sincerely hope you can say you are on track with your finances (or soon to be) after reading this book. Remember, as time goes on, there will be changes, so keep up to date to stay on track. I wish you the very best with your future financial journey, and I'm here if you ever want to take a ride again.

Use these checklists to summarise all the hard work you have done on your journey through *The Money Edit*.

BUDGETING CHECKLIST

☐ **Tally all income** – the more income you have, the more you will enjoy, so don't leave anything out.

☐ **Identify all spending** – go through all your outgoings and separate into essential and enjoyable expenses.

☐ **Use your net income for budgeting** – to get a realistic outcome.

☐ **Average any irregular income** – averaging your income will help you budget better.

☐ **Create a passive income (side hustle)** – turn your passion/ skills into additional income.

☐ **Increase your income** – explore ways you can earn more income while doing what you do.

☐ **Know your worth** – decide on the income you deserve.

☐ **Set excess income aside** – if you earn more than you need set aside 20% for rainy days.

☐ **Compare the market** – aim to keep bills as low as possible by comparing the market.

☐ **Reassess reducing income** – review your budgets if your income has reduced to see what you can afford.

☐ **Set up a money management account** – to help you manage your money effectively.

☐ **Set up direct debits** – for all regular bills.

☐ **Separate your expenses** – have separate accounts for essentials and discretionary spending.

☐ **Set a monthly spending sacrifice** – select one thing you will give up each month and add towards a future goal.

☐ **Continually review your budget** – to help you stay on track, especially in changing circumstances.

Can you think of any others?

SAVING AND INVESTING CHECKLIST

☐ **Set a goal** – decide your WHY for saving or investing.

☐ **Set timescale** – consider how long you will save or invest to achieve your goal.

☐ **Make savings and investments essential** – it should form part of your essential expenses.

☐ **Consider the returns** – decide what return you want to help you choose the right option.

☐ **Choose the right account** – select the appropriate savings or investment account to meet your needs.

☐ **Emergency fund** – build up at least three months of liquid cash in case of emergencies.

☐ **Make use of your ISA allowance** – it's tax-free, so take advantage of it!

☐ **Decide on your attitude to risk** – before you save or invest think about how you feel about risk (low, medium or high).

☐ **Decide on active or passive investment strategy** – what type of investment strategy do you prefer?

☐ **Keep up with future changes** – note down any future changes you expect and how they may affect your plans.

☐ **Financial advice** – decide whether you need support investing or you are confident to do it by yourself.

☐ **Diversify** – make sure you diversify when investing; don't put all your eggs in one basket.

☐ **Keep track** – remember to keep track of your savings and investments and maximise opportunities.

Can you think of any others?

BORROWING AND BUYING PROPERTY CHECKLIST

- **Identify good and bad borrowing** – to help you make the right borrowing choices.
- **Maintain good credit** – keep a review of your credit score and ensure it remains healthy.
- **Establish the right reason for borrowing** – if you can't think of a good reason, avoid borrowing altogether.

☐ **Find the right credit card** – to suit your lifestyle and avoid high interest rates.

☐ **Compare the market** – for the cheapest personal loans.

☐ **Set the date** – for when you want to buy a property.

☐ **Set up a savings account for your deposit** – make a note of how much you need to save, so the goal is clear.

☐ **Create a wish list** – to help you find your dream property with ease.

☐ **Research first time buyer incentives** – get all the help you need to get on the property ladder.

☐ **Decide on your mortgage options** – decide between repayment or interest only, and fixed or variable payments.

☐ **Factor in additional costs** – understand all the costs involved, including post purchase, so there are no surprises.

☐ **Reduce your expenses** – if you are serious about achieving your property goal.

☐ **Get an affordability check** – to understand how much you can borrow.

☐ **Prepare before your mortgage application** – make sure you have all the necessary documentation ready.

☐ **Make an offer** – when you have everything in place – go for it!

Can you think of any others?

FINANCIAL TRANSITIONS CHECKLIST

☐ **Set couple goals** – so your plans are clear and fair for everyone.

☐ **Communicate** – discuss your finances with your partner.

☐ **Deal with unresolved emotions** – emotions can lead to poor financial choices, so seek support first.

☐ **Create a baby budget** – your bundle of joy will come with added costs, so set a budget.

☐ **Teach your children money values** – this is the financial foundation for their future.

☐ **Open a children's account** – start saving for your child from a young age to give them a head start.

☐ **Help your children get on the property ladder** – consider intergenerational mortgages to help support your child to buy their first home.

☐ **Protect your family** – make sure your family are adequately covered should the worst happen.

☐ **Protect your income** – cover yourself if you are unable to work due to an accident or sickness.

☐ **Protect your business** – cover your business against unforeseen events.

☐ **Beware of duplicating insurance policies** – it's so easy to do.

☐ **Review your finances through changing circumstances** – make sure you remain financially stable regardless of the circumstances.

☐ **Take time to heal** – avoid arranging your finances if you are not in the right frame of mind.

☐ **Set a debt plan** – don't let your debt situation get worse.

☐ **Seek financial support through bereavement** – consider all financial support available when coping with the death of a loved one.

☐ **Make a will** – so all your hard work does not go to waste. Decide who you want to inherit your estate and how.

☐ **Identify your net worth** – add up all your assets and subtract all your liabilities to calculate your net worth.

☐ **Create a power of attorney** – so your finances can remain sound even if you're not.

☐ **Set a plan for unexpected lump sums** – so you can see where your money goes instead of wondering where it went.

- ☐ **Make use of free gifts** – if you can gift for free, why not use it?
- ☐ **Utilise investments** – to help reduce inheritance tax.
- ☐ **Put your insurance in trust** – it's simple and cost-effective and will save you thousands of pounds in tax.
- ☐ **Keep a note of normal expenditure** – an easy way to reduce inheritance tax if recorded (see page 189).
- ☐ **Educate your trustees and executors** – if you're leaving your estate plans in someone else's hands, take time to show them where to find everything.
- ☐ **Consider private healthcare** – it's a good idea to arrange some cover to provide quality healthcare if needed.

Can you think of any others?

RETIREMENT CHECKLIST

- ☐ **Set retirement goals** – what does retirement look like for you?
- ☐ **Contribute into a pension** – what you put in is what you get out.
- ☐ **Make use of workplace support** – whether it's a salary sacrifice or your pension contributions being matched, it all helps.
- ☐ **Decide on the age you want to retire** – check your pension plans and see if it's realistic.
- ☐ **Consolidate pensions** – make sure you go through all the pros and cons before you consolidate.
- ☐ **Define a post-career plan** – decide what will stay, go or remain the same after you stop working.

☐ **Assess your spending needs** – go through all outgoings. On average, you will need at least 70% of your pre-retirement income, but aim to be more specific.

☐ **Tally all income** – the more income you have, the more you will enjoy the retirement you deserve, so don't leave anything out.

☐ **Make the most of tax-free cash** – remember it is 25% of your life savings.

☐ **Consider alternative options** – what are your plans A, B and C in retirement? It's worth having multiple options.

☐ **Consider the WHAT IF** – what can be done if you fall short?

☐ **Decide on when you will take your pension** – planning will help you select a suitable date.

☐ **Make a bucket list** – your retirement should be a joyous chapter in your life; go for gold, don't hold back! Set a bucket list of all the things you have dreamed of doing. You will thank yourself later!

Can you think of any others?

You have reached your final destination on your financial journey. Remember to take all the knowledge you have gained throughout *The Money Edit*.

Always remember that your present situation is not your financial destination. The best is yet to come!

> *'Don't follow the path. Go where there is no path and start a trail.'*
> —RUBY BRIDGES

FINANCIAL PLANNING TOOLS

In this section you will find a number of helpful lists and charts to help you create a plan for every stage of your financial life. The following actionable tasks are designed to help you benefit from a more personable approach to your financial journey and be open and honest to overcome financial fears and manage money with confidence. For example, by understanding your income and outgoings, you can gain the financial control you need to take your finances to the next level. Feel free to complete the sections that apply to you. You may also want to work toward increasing income or creating additional income or getting rid of unwanted expenses. Remember, every penny counts! Use these sections at your leisure and remember you can refer back at any time.

Taxes breakdown

Before we explore your income, expenses, assets and liabilities in more detail, it might help to understand the different taxes you might encounter and how they might affect you throughout your lifetime. Here is a breakdown of the most common types of tax.

INCOME TAX

Income tax is the tax you pay on income received. It is levied on employed income, self-employed income, savings interest, investment bonds, income received from rental properties, rent-a-room income and income from pensions. (This list is non-exhaustive, and income tax may apply on other sources of income.) How much income tax you pay in each tax year depends on your income above the personal allowance (the amount of income you can earn each year without paying tax) and how much your income falls within each tax band. There are currently three taxable bands: basic rate tax, higher rate tax and additional rate tax. Income tax is assessed on the income you receive each tax year from 6 April to 5 April. If you are employed, then income tax will be deducted before you are paid. Most other income sources will be taxed following a self-assessment return. If your income is under the personal allowance, there is no tax to pay.

NATIONAL INSURANCE CONTRIBUTIONS (NIC)

You pay mandatory National Insurance if you're 16 or over and are either working or self-employed (earning over a certain level). The National Insurance you pay qualifies for certain benefits and the State Pension. There are different types of National Insurance, known as classes. The type you pay depends on your employment status and earnings. NIC will be deducted from your pay at source and show on your payslip if you are employed. If self-employed, you pay National Insurance through your self-assessment.

DIVIDENDS TAX

You may receive a dividend payment if you own shares in a company. It's common for directors of limited companies to draw dividends above earnings. You do not pay tax on income derived from dividends that falls within your personal allowance. You also get a dividend allowance each year and only pay tax on any excess dividend income. Although dividends tax comes under income tax, the tax charged is different.

CAPITAL GAINS TAX (CGT)

Capital gains tax is a tax on the profit when you sell or dispose of an asset with increased value, such as property. The tax is levied on the gain or profit of the original value when acquired and not the amount received upon sale. Disposing of an asset includes selling an asset, giving an asset away as a gift, swapping an asset for something else or receiving compensation for an asset. Capital gains tax is assessed on gains received each tax year from 6 April to 5 April. You need to report any gains by 31 December in the tax year after you made the gain. There are currently two taxable bands: basic rate tax and higher rate tax (tax charged on property profits differs from other assets gains). Some assets are free of capital gains, such as your main residence. Also, if gains are under the CGT allowance, there is no tax to pay.

INHERITANCE TAX (IHT)

Inheritance tax is a tax on the estate (property, money and possessions) of someone who has died. You will benefit from an increased threshold if you give your home to your children (including adopted, foster or stepchildren) or grandchildren. Gifts made during your lifetime might be subject to inheritance tax if the gift is more than the threshold and a death occurs within seven years of the gift. If you gift a certain proportion of your estate to a charity, you can reduce the amount of IHT you pay. If you're married or in a civil partnership, you benefit from a combined threshold, meaning any unused threshold can be added to the surviving spouse upon death (if married, IHT is only applicable on the second death). Payment for inheritance tax is due by the end of the sixth month after the person dies. There's normally no inheritance tax to pay if the value of your estate is below the threshold.

CORPORATION TAX

You pay corporation tax on profits from doing business as a limited company, a foreign company with a UK branch or office, or a club, cooperative, or other unincorporated association. You don't get a bill for corporation tax, so there are specific things you must do to work out, pay and report your tax. Corporation tax is usually due 12 months after the end of your accounting period and is commonly submitted by an accountant due to the complexities.

Tax is subject to changes; for specific tax charges, please visit www.gov.uk/browse/tax.

Your budget

This section explores your income and outgoings.

INCOME PLANNER

Take a look at this sample income planner. This list is non-exhaustive and may differ depending on your personal income and goals.

Income criteria	Actual income (present)	Target income (future)
Salary	£30,000	£50,000
Earning (self-employed)	£10,000 (side hustle)	£30,000
Royalties	n/a	n/a
Online income	Not yet	Not sure
Pension	n/a	n/a
Property	£10,000	£15,000
State benefits	n/a	n/a
Savings	£10	n/a (I want to invest)
Investment	Not yet	Not sure
Maintenance	n/a	n/a
Grants	n/a	n/a
Redundancy	n/a	n/a
Other	n/a	n/a
Total	£50,010	£95,000

Now try filling in your own income details.

Income criteria	Actual income (present)	Target income (future)
Salary		
Earning (self-employed)		
Royalties		
Online income		
Pension		
Property		
State benefits		
Savings		
Investment		
Maintenance		
Grants		
Redundancy		
Other		
Total		

ESSENTIAL EXPENSES PLANNER

This list is non-exhaustive and may differ depending on your personal expenses (fill in the sections that apply).

HOUSEHOLD	AMOUNT
Mortgage	£
Rent	£
Utilities	£
Council tax	£
Food	£
Telephone	£
Mobile	£
Broadband	£
TV licence	£
Total	£

TRAVEL	AMOUNT
Car fuel	£
Car tax	£
Car MOT	£
Car servicing	£
Electric charging	£
Railcard/rail fares	£
Oyster card	£
Parking tickets	£
Congestion or emissions charge	£
Total	£

DEBTS	AMOUNT
Other mortgages	£
Secured loans	£
Unsecured loans	£
Hire purchase loans	£
Credit cards	£
Buy now pay later	£
Overdraft	£
Warranties	£
Total	£

INSURANCE	AMOUNT
Home insurance	£
Car insurance	£
Life insurance	£
Critical illness	£
Income protection	£
Private health/medical insurance	£
Travel insurance	£
Pet insurance	£
Total	£

FAMILY AND PERSONAL CARE	AMOUNT
Maintenance/child support	£
School fees	£
Nursery fees	£
Clothes	£
Personal care/cosmetics	£
Laundry/dry cleaning	£
Miscellaneous	£
Total	£

SAVINGS AND INVESTMENTS	AMOUNT
Emergency savings	£
General savings	£
Pension	£
Investment	£
Religious savings	£
Partner/group savings	£
Other savings	£
Total	£

ENJOYABLE EXPENSES PLANNER

This section may differ depending on how outgoing you are. List your current spending below, and try to fix a target amount that represents the amount you would like to spend or the amount you can afford.

Criteria	Amount	Target
Sky	£	£
Netflix	£	£
Cleaner	£	£
Music	£	£
Eating out/entertaining	£	£
Socialising	£	£
Holiday/travel	£	£
Hobbies	£	£
Sports/recreation	£	£
Subscriptions	£	£
Shopping (clothes and shoes)	£	£
Hairdresser/grooming	£	£
Beauty treatments	£	£
Make-up	£	£
Birthdays/celebrations	£	£
Parties/clubbing	£	£
Alcohol/tobacco	£	£
Other	£	£
TOTAL	£	£

YOUR BUDGET OUTCOME

Now you have listed all your income and outgoings, it's time to look at what's left over. This section will help you identify your disposable income (income minus expenditure) and your opportunities or options depending on the outcome.

Total income	
Total expenditure	
Disposable income (income minus expenditure)	

- **If your budget is GREEN (money left over after expenses)**
Well done on spending less than you earn! You deserve to pat yourself on the back. It is a great start to building financial freedom. However, you want to ensure you put your excess funds to good use, to help you achieve future goals. (See making use of the leftovers on page 57.)

- **If your budget is AMBER (you spend what you earn)**
To spend all the money you earn, thus saving none or very little in the process, is a category many succumb to. To break the cycle, you need to think differently about money, track your spending and reduce spending where possible if you want to achieve future financial goals. (See my top 10 ways to reduce spending on page 66.)

- **If your budget is RED (you spend more than you earn)**
Consistently spending more than you earn is an easy way to fall into debt and can lead you down the road of financial disaster. The good news is that you can make some swift changes to avoid

remaining in the red and get back on track. It might mean eating out less, shopping smarter or using less energy – whatever it takes to help you reduce spending and save more towards future financial goals. (See ex your expenses and 20 easy ways to reduce your spending on pages 60 and 62).

BUDGET BUDDY

Your budget buddy will help you look at your overall income and expenditure and identify one thing you can sacrifice each month to increase your yearly disposable income and help you save more.

Month	Income	Expense	Sacrifice	Leftovers	Saving
January					
February					
March					
April					
May					
June					
July					
August					
September					
October					
November					
December					

GOAL PRIORITIES LIST

Try listing your goals in priority order to help you laser focus on achieving your money milestones. Once you have completed each section give yourself a big tick!

DAILY

WEEKLY

MONTHLY

QUARTERLY

HALF-YEARLY

YEARLY

LONG-TERM

SAVINGS TRACKER

Now it's time to explore your savings goal (i.e. a car, holiday or business). Decide on what you really want to save for, how much it will cost and when you want to achieve it. Then make a note of every time you save so you can see your success each step of the way.

SAVING FOR:

GOAL DATE:

TOTAL GOAL:

SAVING	DATE

PROPERTY SAVINGS TRACKER

Work out what your monetary property goal is and write it in the goal box. Decide on a set amount you need to save each month to achieve your goal within the required timescale. Use the chart below as an example to track your progress. Every time you save an amount towards your property deposit, add a tick.

Goal: £

£100	£200	£300	£400	£500

Total deposit saved

Target date

PROPERTY WISH LIST

Here is a simple wish list that you can complete when looking for a property. Your wish list should clearly define your needs and wants to make your property search simpler.

CRITERIA	
Target date	
Price range	
Location (city/country)	
Property type (terraced, semi-detached, detached)	
Number of bedrooms	
Garden preference	
Parking preference	
Age of property (i.e. Victorian, new-build)	
Tenure (freehold/leasehold)	
Layout (i.e. open plan, kitchen with separate dining)	
Amenities (tube links, parks, schools, shops)	

DEBT THERMOMETER

Use the debt thermometer to keep track of your progress when trying to clear debt. First, add your total debt owed and the target date you want to clear it by. Every time you pay down towards your debt, update the chart below – until you're completely out of the red (you can do it!)

Target date to clear debt:

- -

%	DEBT GOING DOWN
e.g. 100%	£8,750

TALLY YOUR NET WORTH

It's time to total up your net worth by listing the amount of all your assets (house, car, collectables) and liabilities (debts, mortgage). Once you have the totals, you subtract your liabilities from your assets to work out your net worth. It doesn't matter so much what the outcome is; it's more important that you are aware of it so you can keep track in future.

ASSETS	LIABILITIES
• _____	• _____
• _____	• _____
• _____	• _____
• _____	• _____
• _____	• _____
• _____	• _____
• _____	• _____
• _____	• _____
• _____	• _____
TOTAL £	£

NET WORTH (Assets minus liabilities)	

RETIREMENT GOALS

Take a moment to list the goals you want to achieve in retirement, and what they're likely to cost.

My Retirement Goals	Price Tag

HOW MUCH INCOME WILL YOU
NEED IN RETIREMENT?

Think about what your expenditure will look like in retirement
by breaking down what expenses will go, what will stay and what
will be new.

WAY OUT   **WAY IN**

- - - - - - - - - - - - - - -   - - - - - - - - - - - - - - -

- - - - - - - - - - - - - - -   - - - - - - - - - - - - - - -

- - - - - - - - - - - - - - -   - - - - - - - - - - - - - - -

- - - - - - - - - - - - - - -   - - - - - - - - - - - - - - -

- - - - - - - - - - - - - - -   - - - - - - - - - - - - - - -

STAYING

- -

- -

- -

- -

- -

- -

GLOSSARY

Absolute trust Also referred to as a bare trust, is a trust where the beneficiary is named at the outset and cannot be changed.

Actively managed fund A fund that is actively managed by a fund manager, who selects shares on your behalf for a cost (annual management charge).

Annual allowance The total amount that can be contributed into a pension each tax year receiving tax relief.

Annual equivalent rate (AER) This is the interest rate for a savings account or investment product with more than one compounding period.

Annual management charge The annual charge of actively managed funds, expressed as a percentage of the funds under management.

Annual percentage rate (APR) The official rate used to help you understand the cost of borrowing plus associated fees.

Arrears A legal term for the part of an overdue debt after missing one or more required payments.

Assets Anything of value that can be converted to cash such as shares and property.

Attendance Allowance An amount of money that can be claimed for those over the State Pension age who need regular help with personal care.

Auto-enrolment A government initiative that requires every employer to offer qualifying staff a workplace pension and make set contributions.

Bank of England The Central Bank of the United Kingdom, responsible for issuing banknotes and setting the Bank of England base rate that underpins interest rates (savings and borrowing).

Bank of England base rate The single most important interest rate in the UK is set by the Monetary Policy Committee (MPC), who the government targets to keep inflation low and safe.

Budget A track of income and expenses to improve money management.

Benefit in kind A benefit paid by employers to employees such as company cars, private medical insurance and free loans.

Capital gains tax (CGT) The tax paid on disposal (sale or gift) of an asset's gain after allowance.

Carer's allowance An income benefit (taxable) for people giving regular and substantial care to a disabled or vulnerable person (subject to eligibility).

Cash A common asset for many because it is visible. In terms of investments, cash is often held in 'money markets' (short-term loans between banks and financial institutions).

Commodities These are investments in raw materials dug out of the ground (gold, silver, crude oil) or grown (sugar, coffee beans, wheat).

Compounded interest This is the interest you receive on interest, usually associated with investing.

Contract out This is where members of employer scheme pensions could pay less NI contributions into the state pension.

County court judgment (CCJ) A court order that is registered against you if you fail to pay the money you owe.

Credit scoring A statistical analysis performed by lenders and financial institutions to access a person's creditworthiness.

Credit report The information that determines your credit score, including debts, savings and electoral roll address.

Death in service A tax-free lump sum (typically 2–5 times annual salary) offered by an employer to an employee who dies while employed.

Debit card A payment card that can be used in place of cash to make purchases.

Decreasing term insurance A policy associated with life and critical illness cover that provides a decreasing cover for a fixed period, usually suited to repayment mortgages.

Director The owner of a limited company.

Disability Living Allowance (DLA) A state payment for disabled people, which has been replaced by Personal Independence Payment (PIP). However, it is still applicable to those under 16.

Discretionary trust Also known as a variable trust; this is a trust where the trustees have the flexibility to make changes. Beneficiaries can be grouped, i.e., children or grandchildren.

Diversification An investment strategy that helps reduce risk by investing in a range of asset classes.

Dividend allowance Dividend income you can earn without paying tax.

Emerging markets Investing in developing countries or economies such as China, Brazil, Africa and Russia.

Equity Also known as shares or stocks, is the ownership of an asset, or the value of shares issued by a company. Equities can be subdivided into regions such as UK equities, overseas equities and emerging markets.

Equity release A way of releasing cash from your home without having to move (risk involved).

Financial adviser A qualified professional who recommends financial products based on an individual's personal circumstances and goals. There are two types: independent and restricted.

Financial Conduct Authority (FCA) The body that regulates financial organisations and financial advisers to provide confidence to consumers and businesses.

Financial Services Compensation Scheme (FSCS) Protects customers' savings and investments if a company fails by providing compensation (limits apply).

Financial Ombudsman Service (FOS) Deals with financial complaints and provides settlement between the complainant and financial service company.

Fixed interest rate An unchanging rate charged on a liability, such as a loan or a mortgage.

Forex The act of buying or selling currency on the foreign exchange market.

FTSE 100 An index that represents the UK's 100 largest listed companies (shares).

Furlough A temporary leave of absence from work due to an economic condition affecting the whole country.

Government bonds Also known as gilts or corporate bonds, this is the process of lending money to the government or a large corporation, almost like an IOU. In return they pay back interest (coupon) after a set period.

Guarantor A financial term describing an individual who promises to pay a borrower's debt if the borrower defaults on their loan obligation, such as rent or mortgage.

Income tax The tax paid on income received after personal allowance.

Inflation The measured rate of average prices known as a basket of goods and services. The two measures are the Retail Price Index (RPI) and the Consumer Price Index (CPI).

Inheritance tax (IHT) The tax paid on the net estate (assets minus liabilities) on death after nil rate band.

Interest-only mortgage A home loan including only the interest on the amount you have borrowed; at the end of the term the original amount borrowed will remain.

Investment bond A life insurance policy that can hold investments in a tax efficient manner. You can take tax deferred withdrawals up to 5% each year (risk involved).

Investment trusts Collective investments vehicles that are set up as companies selling shares. The money raised is invested in a range of assets such as shares, gilts and bonds.

Joint tenant A person who holds an estate or property jointly with one or more parties, the share of each passing to the other or others on death.

Land registry An official record of information on who owns particular land and property and whether money is owed.

Level term insurance A policy associated with life and critical illness cover that provides a set cover for a fixed period, usually suited to interest-only mortgages.

Liabilities Something a person or a company owes, usually money.

Lifetime allowance The total limit you can build up in a pension over your lifetime.

Limited company A company separated from shareholders offering limited liability.

Loan to value The ratio used by lenders to assess the loan amount to the value of the asset.

Money coach Someone who guides individuals through financial decisions and helps identify and achieve financial goals.

Money mentor Supports individuals through financial decisions based on personal experience and expertise.

Money purchase annual allowance Limits the amount that can be contributed to a money purchase scheme after drawing a pension.

Mortgage offer An official confirmation from the lender to the buyer, outlining the arrangements of the mortgage.

Money therapist Combines financial guidance with emotional support to help individuals cope with financial stress.

Negative equity When a property's value is less than the outstanding mortgage.

Nil rate band The IHT threshold below which there is no tax to pay. The amount increases in line with CPI.

Open-ended investment contracts (OEIC) A type of investment fund in the UK that is structured to invest in stocks and other securities.

The pension protection fund A statutory fund in the UK, intended to protect members if their defined benefits pension fund becomes insolvent.

Passive managed fund Also known as index or tracker fund; an investment intended to replicate the return of a market index (i.e. FTSE 100) without human intervention.

Paternity pay A continuous pay (usually one to two weeks) for men who are off work to support their spouse after having a baby (subject to eligibility).

Personal allowance The amount of income you can receive before you pay tax.

Property deposit The amount of money paid as a percentage of the full property price.

Repayment mortgage A home loan including capital and interest; at the end of the term the mortgage loan is cleared.

Secured loan This is when you borrow money that is secured against an asset you own, usually your home.

SERPs or State Second Pension (S2P) A pension arrangement for people who have contracted out of the Additional State Pension.

Service charge These are charges payable by the leaseholder to the landlord for the services provided under the lease terms, such as maintenance, repair and sometimes (exterior) improvement.

Shareholder An owner of shares in a company.

Sole trader A person who runs a business as an individual, also known as self-employed.

Stamp Duty Land Tax A tax paid on land purchases over a certain threshold.

Statutory Maternity Pay (SMP) A payment made by employers to employees on leave expecting a baby. SMP is paid for up to 39 weeks (subject to eligibility).

Statutory Sick Pay (SSP) A state income benefit an employer pays to an employee who is sick and unable to work. It's paid by your employer for up to 28 weeks (subject to eligibility).

Store card A credit card you can only use with one high street chain or group.

Subprime lending The practice of lending to borrowers with low credit ratings at typically higher than average rates.

Tax-free childcare A regular payment from the government (replaced childcare vouchers in 2018) paid to a parent for each child to help with childcare cost (subject to eligibility).

Tax-free lump sum Also referred to as pension commencement lump sum. You can usually take up to 25% of the amount built up in any pension as a *tax-free lump sum*.

Tenants in common Refers to when each owner has a distinct share of the property. There are no rights of survivorship afforded to any account holders.

Unit trust A type of mutual fund managed by fund managers to achieve a specific return. It pools together money from various investors to invest in assets like shares and bonds.

Universal Credit A payment to help with living costs for those who are on a low income, out of work or unable to work (subject to eligibility).

Unsecured loan Also called a personal loan, it doesn't require any collateral. You borrow money from a bank or other lenders and agree to make regular payments (including interest) until the loan is repaid in full.

Variable interest rate An interest rate on a loan or security fluctuates over time because it is based on an underlying benchmark interest rate or index that changes periodically.

Yield A measure of the return to a holder of the security or asset.

RESOURCES

WEBSITES

CHECK YOUR CREDIT RATING

Check My File
www.checkmyfile.com

ClearScore
www.clearscore.com

Equifax
www.equifax.couk

Experian
www.experian.co.uk

DEBT

Advice UK
Independent free advice around money and debt.
www.adviceuk.org.uk

Citizens Advice
Online free debt and money advice.
www.citizensadvice.org.uk

Samaritans
A registered charity that provides emotional support.
www.samaritans.org

Step Change
A debt charity, offering expert debt advice and fee-free debt
    management.
www.stepchange.org

Turn 2 Us
A charity that helps people in financial hardship gain access to
    welfare benefits, charitable grants and support services.
www.turn2us.org.uk

FINANCIAL LITERACY

Bank of England
A good resource for information about the current financial landscape.
www.bankofengland.co.uk

GOV.UK
For money and tax guidance and support.
www.gov.uk

Investopedia
The world's leading source of financial content.
www.investopedia.com

Money Advice Service & Money Helper
Free and impartial help with money and pensions.
www.moneyhelper.org.uk

Money Saving Expert
Free money savings website.
www.moneysavingexpert.com

This Is Money
Personal finance and investing news, advice and guides.
www.thisismoney.co.uk

Trust Pilot
Customer review site.
uk.trustpilot.com

TWC Personal Finance Blog
Helps you get on track of your finances regardless of where you
    are on your journey.
www.makalagreen.com/blog

Which?
Customer review site.
www.which.co.uk

YouGov
UK-based market research and opinion polling platform.
www.yougov.co.uk

MONEY MANAGEMENT

Confused
Price comparison site.
www.confused.com

GoCompare
Price comparison site.
www.gocompare.com

MoneySuperMarket
Price comparison site.
www.moneysupermarket.com

Trolley
Compare products across supermarkets and shops.
www.trolley.co.uk

The Money Charity
Helps people manage money and increase their financial wellbeing.
www.themoneycharity.org.uk

Trustnet
A free daily updated analysis and price/performance data on all
Investments and Pensions.
www.trustnet.com

Uswitch
Price comparison site.
www.uswitch.com

PENSIONS

Check Your State Pension Forecast
To see how much State Pension you could get, and when.
www.gov.uk/check-state-pension

Compare Annuity
Annuity comparison site.
www.compare.annuity.uk.com

Find Pension Contact Details
Use this service to find and search for lost pensions.
www.gov.uk/find-pension-contact-details

Money Advice Service & Money Helper
Free and impartial help with money and pensions.
www.moneyhelper.org.uk

Retirement Line
Annuity comparison site.
www.retirementline.co.uk

The Money & Pensions Service
A body sponsored by the Department for Work and Pensions.
www.moneyandpensionsservice.org.uk

The Pensions Advisory Service (TPAS)
Free information and advice about state, company and personal
    pensions.
www.pensionsadvisoryservice.org.uk

Pension Wise
Government-approved free impartial help with money and pensions.
www.moneyhelper.org.uk/en

PROPERTY

Money Helper
Find out how much you can afford to borrow for your new house.
www.moneyhelper.org.uk/en/homes/buying-a-home/mortgage-
    affordability-calculator

Rightmove
Property search site.
www.rightmove.co.uk

Stamp Duty Land Tax (SDLT) Calculator
This calculator can be used to work out the SDLT payable for
property purchases.
www.tax.service.gov.uk/calculate-stamp-duty-land-tax

Zoopla
Property search site.
www.zoopla.co.uk

FINANCIAL REGULATORS AND COMPENSATION SCHEMES

Financial Conduct Authority (FCA)
The Financial Services and Markets Regulator.
www.fca.org.uk

Financial Ombudsman Service (FOS)
Free, fair service that settles financial complaints.
www.financial-ombudsman.org.uk

Financial Services Compensation Scheme (FSCS)
Protects savings and investments if financial firms fail.
www.fscs.org.uk

Pension Protection Fund
Protects people with defined benefit pensions when an employer
becomes insolvent.
www.ppf.co.uk

Prudential Regulation Authority (PRA)
Regulates and supervises financial services.
www.bankofengland.co.uk/prudential-regulation

*Limits and caps apply to compensation schemes and protection funds.

TAX

GOV.UK
For money and tax guidance and support.
www.gov.uk

APPS

Emma
Finimize
Money Dashboard
Moneyhub
Monzo

PODCASTS

FT Money Clinic with Clare Barrett
Money Box
The Meaningful Money
The Which? Money Podcast
Your Financial Journey

RADIO

BBC Radio 4's *Money Box*
BBC Radio 5 Live's *Wake Up to Money*
BBC Radio London
talkRADIO

NEWSPAPERS AND MAGAZINES

Financial Times
FinTech Magazine
Investors Chronicle
MoneyWeek
The Daily Express
The Daily Telegraph
The *Economist*
The *Guardian*
The Times

ACKNOWLEDGEMENTS

I now know the process of birthing a book, and it has been one of the most extraordinary experiences in my adult life, one which I am most grateful to have had. However, this book would not be possible without the help of countless people who supported me along the way.

My parents for laying the foundation and teaching me to value life and money – I love you both to bits!

My husband for continually pushing me to go above and beyond and supporting me throughout. You are my rock, and I love and appreciate you always.

My children for inspiring me to be the greatest version of myself – Mummy loves you dearly.

My older sisters for gifting me many books and encouraging and believing in me from the start – I love you both.

My younger brothers, who always ask me for book recommendations (here's one for you!), you have all encouraged me to write this book – big sis loves you.

My BIG family and friends for all the encouragement and support – you know it's always love.

Marilyn Messik, for inspiring me to write this book and for all your hard work, support and continuous encouragement (I couldn't have done it without you!).

My amazing team; Bev James, thank you for giving me an opportunity to release this gift and for being the inspiration that you are; Tom Wright, Morwenna Loughman and Emily Prosser, for believing in me, seeing my vision and working tirelessly to make my dream come true.

Charlotte Belle Tobin, Megan Davis and Mollie Tant, you ladies have been nothing but amazing, thank you all for your ongoing hard work and aligning your efforts with my determination to demystify financial planning. Thereasa Morgan, thank you for putting up with me over the years and always holding the fort.

My clients, colleagues and cheerleaders for trusting, believing and supporting me on my mission; I have gained so much value from you all and cherish your contribution.

My financial industry family, who have paved the way for me and inspired my journey. Irene Agunbiade, Louise O'Kane, Sam Seaton and Emmanuel Asuquo, just to name a few.

My Instagram family (The WealthCheckers), for your encouragement, likes, love and shares, I am forever grateful.

Finally, my sincere thanks to the entire team at Yellow Kite, my editor Clare Sayer, Emma Knight, Holly Whitaker, Olivia Nightingall and Carolyn Thorne, for bringing the book to life.

Without all your unswerving faithfulness, dedication and support, this book may not have been possible. I am grateful for the guidance, encouragement and patience I have had while writing, running a business, and balancing family life; it has been an intense, challenging, exciting journey.

I am so humbled and blessed to be surrounded by people I love and cherish and to be able to work with committed, talented and passionate people to make this book a reality.

ABOUT THE AUTHOR

© Dom Martin

Makala Green is an award-winning chartered financial expert, businesswoman, financial speaker, podcaster, and wealth coach. She has over 18 years' experience financially transforming individuals and businesses across a diverse sector of money management, investment planning and property acquisition.

She is the founder of Green Wealth Planning and The Wealth Check, a platform created to help make wealth simple and give people the tools they need to confidently take control of their money and plan their financial journey. She has partnered with multi-million-pound companies such as Waitrose, John Lewis, and Metro Bank and featured in various publications such as The Female Lead, Financial Times, Glamour, Stylist, Yahoo Finance, Huffington Post and FinTech Magazine.

INDEX